Landlor
Letters

Adam Church

Landlord's Letters
by Adam Church

1st edition 2005
   Reprinted 2006
2nd edition 2007

© 2007 Lawpack Publishing

Lawpack Publishing Limited
76–89 Alscot Road
London SE1 3AW

www.lawpack.co.uk

ISBN: 978-1-905261-55-0

Exclusion of Liability and Disclaimer

Contents

All the letters included in this book can also be downloaded free of charge from our website. To access them, all you have to do is register on the Lawpack website at www.lawpack.co.uk and then click on the web enablement logo on our homepage. You then enter the activation code printed below when requested.

Registration code: **B6523501105**

About the author

Since graduating from university in 1998, Adam Church has worked extensively in the property industry and has offered his property management services through both independent and corporate offices in the South West of England. In addition to his property experience, he has qualifications from the Guild of Letting and Management and the Association of Residential Letting Agents. He now works mainly from his home in Bristol where he writes full time and offers independent advice to private landlords of residential tenancies.

Introduction

As a landlord you have a great deal of responsibility. On a daily basis you face juggling a business-like attitude whilst complying with ever-changing legislation as well as dealing with challenging tenant issues!

Keeping all of these balls in the air can be difficult. Whilst a good understanding of your legal responsibilities will help you to remain within the law, knowing how to communicate effectively with your tenant will ensure that you implement your duties in accordance with Government regulations and at the same time maintain a healthy working relationship with your tenant.

Many landlords have, because of a lack of understanding on how to communicate with their tenants, found problems that have escalated way beyond necessity. In cases where landlords think that they have followed their legal responsibilities correctly, failure to communicate effectively with their tenants has affected their chances to regain possession of their properties, even when the tenants have been in breach of the terms of their agreements.

Being let down by inaccurate, misleading or a complete lack of effective communication can be time consuming and cause financial losses.

This book has been created, therefore, to provide landlords of residential tenancies with a practical guide to many of the instances where written communication should be sent to the tenant. It demonstrates, with useful information, tips and facts, when letters should be written and why it's important to correspond accordingly with the tenant. Also, included within the book are over 80 helpful letter templates. These have been designed to make it easier for landlords to send clear, accurate information without personal or unnecessary comments which can cause inflamed emotional situations and lead to poor landlord and tenant relationships.

Whilst this book forms a comprehensive tool for landlords in communicating with tenants and can be used in association with a variety of different tenancy agreements, it should not be considered as a guide to the entire lettings process. There are books available, such as Tessa Shepperson's excellent *Residential Lettings* (also published by Lawpack), which explains how to create and manage short-term residential lettings and I recommend that landlords refer to such guides to suit their purposes.

If you're unsure of a situation or you have a specific problem, you should seek independent legal advice rather than rely solely on information contained within this book.

My thanks go to my editor, Jamie Ross, for giving me the opportunity to write this book. My professional experiences in the lettings industry have been the inspiration behind this project and in addition to the many landlords that I have been fortunate enough to work with, I would also like to thank Benjamin and Ruth Dembo, who, although not directly linked with this book, helped me understand the importance of effective communication and maintaining good landlord and tenant relationships early in my career.

Many thanks also go to my wife Helen for her love and support throughout this project.

Adam Church

CHAPTER 1

Vetting your tenant

So you've bought your property, you've got permission from your lender to let it and you're ready to be a landlord. The only thing you need now is a tenant!

Finding the right tenant for your investment can be time consuming and labour intensive, but, like many things, if it's done correctly from the start, you can save a lot of money later on. If you don't take the time to reference potential new tenants thoroughly, you could be leaving yourself open to uncreditworthy or dishonest tenants who may not pay the rent and could leave you with damages.

Some tenants will try to find a property with a private landlord rather than go through a professional agency because they are less likely to be referenced if they avoid agents. These are the tenants it's most important for you to reference and they could be heading your way!

A lot of the paperwork involved with running a tenancy comes before an agreement is signed. If a potential tenant goes to a professional lettings agent and wants to rent your property, he will be asked to fill in an application form. The agent will then send out reference letters for the applicant and wait for satisfactory written responses. Only on successful completion of the application will the applicant even be offered the chance to rent your property.

An agent will try to find out as much information as possible about the tenant in order to secure your investment. Knowing where to get this information and what questions to ask will help you, as a private landlord, to reference your own applicants successfully.

The application form

 The **TENANCY APPLICATION FORM (1.1)** asks your applicant to provide all the relevant information so that you can carry out as thorough a referencing procedure as possible. Clarify which references you require with the applicant at the viewing stage and make sure each applicant completes the form in full and signs it where required.

The first step is to acquire all of the applicant's immediate personal details, such as his name and contact information. If you want to get in touch with your applicant during the referencing procedure, you need to know who he is and where you can get hold of him.

When trying to find a secure tenant there are three or four reliable references that you should expect to carry out:

Previous landlord

If your applicant is currently in rented accommodation, you will need to contact his landlord to find out if the tenancy has been conducted in a satisfactory manner and if he has paid the rent on time. If there have been any problems during the tenancy, detailed information about this will help you to make an informed decision as to whether the applicant is suitable for your property, particularly if there are reports by the previous/current landlord of damage. Ideally, you should try to obtain details of the applicant's past three years in rented accommodation and apply for references from all his relevant landlords.

 PREVIOUS LANDLORD'S REFERENCE (1.2)

Employer

The most secure tenants are often those in full-time, permanent employment with a salary that is in proportion with the amount of rent you are asking. The applicant's employer should be able to confirm his salary and how long he has been with the company. Look out for applicants who are in a probationary period or in temporary employment as these contracts can be terminated quickly and could leave your tenant without any money coming in to pay the rent. Again, try to obtain information for the last three years of your applicant's employment history.

 EMPLOYER'S REFERENCE (1.3)

Financial status and history

There are a number of ways that you can obtain financial references for your applicant and you can use any of the following methods when deciding on the right tenant for your property:

- **Bank reference**

  You can write to the applicant's bank requesting a financial reference.

 BANK REFERENCE (1.4)

In order for the bank to provide you with this information, it's likely that you must have separate written consent from the applicant. You should send this to the bank along with the reference request.

 APPLICANT'S AUTHORISATION TO OBTAIN BANK REFERENCE (1.5)

- **Credit search**

  There are specialist online companies available that will process a credit suitability search on your behalf which will take into account any adverse credit history that the applicant may have had. These can be obtained online for a small fee.

- **Bank statements**

  You can ask your applicant to provide you with copies of his last three months' bank account statements. This will give you the opportunity to see how the applicant manages cash flow and if there are any payments that haven't been honoured by his bank due to insufficient funds, etc.

Personal/character

In many instances the personal or character referee that the applicant provides will usually be a friend or colleague who is unlikely to give any detrimental information about him. In this respect the reference doesn't provide a great deal of insight or security and shouldn't be considered as iron-clad. You may find, however, that any positive feelings you had towards the applicant are confirmed and if you have asked the applicant for a character referee with a managerial or high-ranking position, this can offer a little more peace of mind when you come to make your decision.

 PERSONAL REFERENCE (1.6)

Tip

There are specific rules and guidelines in place regarding obtaining and using personal information which you need to be aware of when seeking references for your applicant. You shouldn't disclose personal information to anyone other than those the applicant has authorised you to deal with, nor should you provide your applicant with copies of any of the references that you have obtained unless you have written consent from the referee. If in doubt, you should check with your local Data Protection office or go to www.ico.gov.uk for more information.

There may be instances when you will be unable to carry out the standard references above because the applicant may:

- be selling his own property;
- own a property and be in the process of separating from his partner;
- be living at home with his parents;
- be out of/unable to work;
- be in receipt of Housing Benefit or looking for employment;
- be self-employed or a registered company;
- be from overseas.

The Tenancy Application Form takes into account some of these scenarios and will give you the opportunity to get a good picture of the applicant's current circumstances. If your applicant is self-employed or is a registered company, then you may wish to obtain an **ACCOUNTANT'S OR SOLICITOR'S REFERENCE (1.7)** or a **TRADE REFERENCE (1.8)**, which may act as a kind of character reference. However, the information provided should come from somebody with a good understanding of the applicant's ability to meet his financial commitments.

Accepting an applicant subject to conditions

Make it clear to your applicant from the very beginning that until you have obtained satisfactory information about him, you will be unable to make a decision about whether or not you can offer him a tenancy. To avoid confusion and to clarify what will be required of the applicant before he is able to move into your property, it's worthwhile giving him a letter, **ACCEPTANCE OF OFFER TO TAKE A TENANCY (SUBJECT TO CONDITIONS) (1.9)**, with the Tenancy Application Form detailing all this information. This will tell the applicant how much money he will have to pay when he signs the agreement.

Tip

Give your applicant a sample copy of the tenancy agreement with his Tenancy Application Form. Encourage the applicant to air any questions or problems he has regarding the tenancy agreement before the start date. This will cut down on time spent going through paperwork on the move-in day.

Considering an applicant

When you are considering an applicant for your property **you** will ultimately make the decision as to whether he will be a suitable tenant. You shouldn't discriminate against race, religion or disability, but you do have the right not to offer a tenancy where you have been unable to obtain a satisfactory amount of security from the applicant or if you feel that he isn't the right tenant for you.

If your applicant is unable to complete the Application Form in full or the references that you have received are not satisfactory for any reason, you may, if you still wish to proceed with the applicant, try to seek other forms of security. These may include asking the applicant whether he can pay the first fixed term of the tenancy in advance or to supply a guarantor who you can reference in the same way.

Preparing for the tenancy

At this stage there are a number of things you will have to do to ensure that you are fully prepared for the start of a new tenancy, which may include:

- **Preparing an Inventory and Schedule of Condition**

  (A document which clearly details the contents and condition of the property which your tenant must sign on the move-in day.)

- **Key cutting**

  (Enough for each tenant so that you both hold complete sets.)

- **Ensuring you have an up-to-date Landlord's Gas Safety Certificate**

(In compliance with the Gas Safety (Installation and Use) Regulations 1998 all gas appliances supplied must be checked by a Corgi-registered plumber and a certificate obtained. A copy of this certificate should be given to your tenant on the day he moves in.)

It can often be difficult to keep track of everything that's going on, so it's useful to keep a simple list that shows you all the jobs you need to do and lets you tick them off as you go.

 LANDLORD'S CHECKLIST (1.10)

The check-in

If the references have all come back satisfactorily and you're happy to proceed, you need to contact your applicant to let him know what needs to happen next. The best place to meet an applicant to carry out a handover is at the property itself. This will also give you the chance to go through the inventory, take meter readings, collect any money owing in cleared funds and give the keys to the tenant. Advising your applicant in writing when you want to do this will give him a chance to prepare everything he needs to ensure that the handover goes without a hitch.

CONFIRMATION OF SATISFACTORY REFERENCES AND APPOINTMENT TO CHECK IN (1.11)

Collecting money

On the day that your tenant moves into the property you will need to ensure that you have collected all of the initial money (such as the deposit) owed in cleared funds and to make sure that provision has been made for the payment of rent as per your agreement.

Note

In this day and age lots of people like to pay for things with credit or debit cards rather than using cash, but, as a private landlord, you are unlikely to have the technology to process a payment in this way. Most tenants will be aware of this, but some will try to give you a cheque to settle their first account payment. This is fine as long as you have had time to put it in your bank and it has cleared into your account.

Make it clear to your applicant that without cleared funds on the day he will be unable to take occupancy. If your applicant is concerned about security, he can ask his bank to create a banker's draft to be made out in your name. This money is taken directly from the applicant's account and the cheque is guaranteed to clear. It also comes with security if the applicant loses the cheque or if it's stolen. Alternatively, you could give the applicant your bank account details and he can transfer the money to you, making sure that there is enough time allowed for the money to reach your account before the start date of the agreement. Don't allow a tenant to move into your property until you have the money!

If your applicant pays you in cash, it's reasonable to give him a **TENANT'S RECEIPT (1.12)** to confirm the amount he has paid and what the money was for. It's good practice to give a receipt to your tenant for any cash or cheque payments that he might make to you over the course of the tenancy. This process demonstrates a professional attitude and gives the tenant the opportunity to keep a record of payments made to you should he need to provide information to accountants or if he wants to maintain good financial housekeeping!

Undoubtedly the most efficient way for your tenant to pay you rent is directly from his bank account into yours. A tenant will promise to set this up if you give him your account details, but it's a good idea to take care of this yourself at the property before you give the tenant the keys. If you present the tenant with a prepared **STANDING ORDER MANDATE (1.13)** and ask him to fill in his personal details, you can make sure the payment is arranged by sending it (or dropping it off) to the tenant's bank.

Explain to your tenant that the money is likely to leave his account a few working days before the date the rent is due in order for it to reach your account in time. This way the tenant can ensure that he has sufficient funds in the account to make the payment and it will avoid arguments when your tenant asks why you collected the rent three days early!!

Tenancy deposit protection

Don't forget that new laws came into place on 6 April 2007 ordering landlords to safeguard the tenant's deposit in one of three Government-approved schemes. If the tenancy began after this date, you must register with one of the schemes and notify your tenant in the prescribed written form within 14 days of taking the tenant's deposit or you could face serious penalties. See Chapter 7 for more details.

Welcome to your new home

You are about to hand over your investment to another person for an agreed period of time so it's definitely worth making him feel at home and assuring him from the start that you care about the property and him living in it.

Don't forget...

Make a good first impression. One of the reasons there is so much legal protection for tenants today is because of rogue landlords who, in the past, have failed to uphold their obligations. Lots of tenants, especially the good ones, can be wary of landlords because of horror stories they might have read in the press or from personal experiences. Do what you can from the beginning to ensure that you and your tenant have a good relationship and this will make the process of renting your property a much simpler one.

Make sure that your new tenant feels comfortable that everything he needs to know about the property has been made available. You shouldn't expect to have to show him how everything works as this could be extremely time consuming, but you should ensure that relevant manuals and instruction booklets (including any warranty information) is made available. A **WELCOME LETTER (1.14)** presented in a folder with anything you feel is relevant for the tenant's needs is a good way to settle any first-day nerves that either party may have and gives the impression that you are a fair and approachable landlord…which of course you are!

1.1 TENANCY APPLICATION FORM

Property address applied for: _____

_____

Rent: £ _____Rental period: _____(months)

Is this a joint application?: ☐ Yes ☐ No

Start date: _____ (TBC)

Name in full: _____

Current address: _____

_____

Tel: (H) _____ (W) _____

Email: _____

Are you a: ☐ Homeowner ☐ Private tenant
          ☐ Living with relatives ☐ Other

Dates at current address:

From: _____To: _____

Reason for leaving: _____

Provide details of previous addresses and dates of occupation for last three years (*continue on separate sheet if necessary*)

_____

_____

_____

_____

_____

Name and address of current landlord:_____

_____

Tel: (H) _____ (W) _____

Email: _____

Name and address of current employer:_____

_____

Tel: _____ Fax: _____

Email: _____

Position held: _____

Date employment commenced: _____

Contact name:_____ Position: _____

1.1 TENANCY APPLICATION FORM (continued)

Your salary (please include any bonus, etc.): _____

National Insurance number:_____

Are you: ☐ Full time ☐ Part time ☐ Temporary
☐ Self-employed ☐ Company let

Bank name and address: _____

_____

Account in the name of: _____

Account number: _____

Sort code: _____

For company lets or self-employed tenants only

Accountant's or solicitor's name: _____

Address:_____

_____

_____

Tel: _____ Fax: _____

Email:_____

For company lets or self-employed tenants only

Name or trade reference (if applicable): _____

Address:_____

_____

_____

Tel: _____Fax: _____

Email:_____

Name and address of personal reference:_____

_____

_____

Tel: (H) _____ (W) _____

Email: _____

Relationship to you: _____

Next of kin's name and address: _____

_____

_____

Tel: (H) _____ (W) _____

Email: _____

1.1 TENANCY APPLICATION FORM (continued)

Relationship to you: _____

Declaration

I hereby authorise you to contact those named in this application for references. I understand that you will require personal information as detailed in this form and give consent for this to be obtained. I declare that the information I have provided here is to the best of my knowledge true and accurate at the time of completion. I may be asked to provide further authorisation for references to be provided and accept this. Should you be unable to obtain satisfactory references I acknowledge that my application may be refused. I also accept that due to the confidential nature of this application I will not be permitted access to the references or be given any explanation should my references prove unsatisfactory.

Name: _____

Signature: _____

Date: _____

Please ensure that this form is completed in full and returned within three days in order for your application to be considered.

1.2 PREVIOUS LANDLORD'S REFERENCE

A. Landlord
76–89 Alscot Road, London SE1 2EA
020 7394 4040

A. P. Landlord
20 Stapleford Avenue, London SW1 3WJ

Date: *1 December 2006*

Dear *A.P. Landlord*

Re: *A. Tenant and his previous property, 12 Brighton Walk, London W1 7AB*

I am writing to advise you that the above named has made an application to take a tenancy with me and has given your details as the previous landlord.

In order to process the application successfully, I kindly request that you complete the following information, sign and return it to me in the stamped-addressed envelope provided as soon as possible. All information will be treated in the strictest of confidence.

1. The length of the tenancy.

2. The amount of rent.

3. Was the rent always paid on time?

4. Were there any problems during the tenancy (please give details)?

5. Were there any deductions from the tenant's deposit?

6. Would you rent to this tenant again?

Thank you for your assistance in this matter.

Yours sincerely

Landlord: *A. Landlord*

Name: Sign:

Date:

1.3 EMPLOYER'S REFERENCE

A. Landlord
76–89 Alscot Road, London SE1 2EA
020 7394 4040

A. Employer
17 Battle Road, London E17 2AP

Date: *1 December 2006*

Dear *A. Employer*

Re: *A. Tenant*

I am writing to advise you that the above named has made an application to take a tenancy with me and has given your details as his current employer.

In order to process the application successfully, I kindly request that you complete the following information, sign and return it in the stamped-addressed envelope provided as soon as possible with a copy of your company letterhead. All information will be treated in the strictest of confidence.

1. The start date of employment.

2. The employee's position.

3. The employee's salary.

4. Is the contract permanent or temporary?

5. Is the employee in a probationary period?

6. The expiry date of the probationary period (if applicable).

Thank you for your assistance in this matter.

Yours sincerely

Landlord: *A. Landlord*

Name: Position Held:

Sign: Date:

1.4 BANK REFERENCE

A. Landlord
76–89 Alscot Road, London SE1 2EA
020 7394 4040

A. Bank
34 Crawley Street, London N7 2AP

Date: *1 December 2006*

Dear *A. Bank*

Re: *A. Tenant, Account No. 0123456, Sort Code 21-00-78*

I am writing to advise you that the above named has made an application to take a tenancy with me and has given your details to provide a financial reference.

In order to process the application successfully, I kindly request that you make the necessary enquiries with your client's account and respond quoting *10 Alscot Road and A. Tenant.*

All information will be treated in the strictest of confidence and I enclose a copy of the applicant's signed authorisation.

Thank you for your assistance in this matter.

Yours sincerely

Landlord: *A. Landlord*

1.5 APPLICANT'S AUTHORISATION TO OBTAIN BANK REFERENCE

I/we _____

_____

Authorise _____ Plc.

To provide a financial reference, in respect of my/our application for a tenancy, to: [*Insert name and address*]

_____

_____

_____

I/we understand that there may be a charge for this service and I/we agree to this fee being deducted from our account accordingly.

Signed:_____

Date: _____

1.6 PERSONAL REFERENCE

A. Landlord
76–89 Alscot Road, London SE1 2EA
020 7394 4040

A. Reference
72 Northwich Way, London NW3 7EP

Date: *1 December 2006*

Dear *A. Reference*

Re: *A. Tenant*

I am writing to advise you that the above named has made an application to take a tenancy with me and has given your details to provide a personal/ character reference.

In order to process the application successfully, I kindly request that you complete the information below, sign and return it in the stamped-addressed envelope provided as soon as possible. All information provided will be treated in the strictest of confidence.

1. Your relationship to the applicant.

2. How long have you known the applicant?

3. Do you consider the applicant to be trustworthy?

4. Is there any reason why a tenancy should not be granted to the applicant?

Thank you for your assistance in this matter.

Yours sincerely

Landlord: *A. Landlord*

Name: Sign:

Date:

1.7 ACCOUNTANT'S/SOLICITOR'S REFERENCE (FOR SELF-EMPLOYED OR COMPANY TENANTS)

A. Landlord
76–89 Alscot Road, London SE1 2EA
020 7394 4040

A. Solicitor
45 Mill Road, London SW13 4UB

Date: *1 December 2006*

Dear *A. Solicitor*

Re: *A. Tenant*

I am writing to advise you that the above named has made an application to take a tenancy with me and has given your details to provide a reference.

In order to process the application successfully, I kindly request that you complete the information below, sign and return it in the stamped-addressed envelope provided as soon as possible. All information provided will be treated in the strictest of confidence.

1. Your relationship to the applicant.

2. How long have you known the applicant?

3. Do you consider the applicant to be trustworthy?

4. Is there any reason why a tenancy should not be granted to the applicant?

Thank you for your assistance in this matter.

Yours sincerely

Landlord: *A. Landlord*

Name: Sign:

Date:

1.8 TRADE REFERENCE (FOR SELF-EMPLOYED OR COMPANY TENANTS)

A. Landlord
76–89 Alscot Road, London SE1 2EA
020 7394 4040

A. Trade
20 Heath Street, London NW7 2UV

Date: *1 December 2006*

Dear *A. Trade*

Re: *A. Tenant*

I am writing to advise you that the above named has made an application to take a tenancy with me and has given your details to provide a trade reference.

In order to process the application successfully, I kindly request that you complete the information below, sign and return it in the stamped-addressed envelope provided as soon as possible. All information provided will be treated in the strictest of confidence.

1. Your relationship to the applicant.

2. How long have you known the applicant?

3. Do you consider the applicant to be trustworthy?

4. Is there any reason why a tenancy should not be granted to the applicant?

Thank you for your assistance in this matter.

Yours sincerely

Landlord: *A. Landlord*

Name: Sign:

Date:

1.9 ACCEPTANCE OF OFFER TO TAKE A TENANCY (SUBJECT TO CONDITIONS)

A. Landlord
76–89 Alscot Road, London SE1 2EA
020 7394 4040

A. Tenant
98 Newcastle Street, London W12 8EL

Date: *12 December 2006*

Dear *A. Tenant*

Re: *10 Alscot Road, London SE1 3EJ*

I am pleased to confirm that your offer to take a tenancy at the above property to commence on *1 January 2007* has been accepted subject to the following conditions:

1. All Applicants complete in full, sign and return the enclosed Application Form within a period of no more than three days.

2. References are returned showing no signs of adverse credit history or unsatisfactory performance during the term of any previous tenancies.

3. A convenient appointment is arranged and takes place on the agreed start date of the contract where all tenants meet and sign the tenancy agreement.

4. The sum of the rent being £400 will be payable in advance on a *monthly* basis.

5. A Security Deposit is to be paid in the sum of £800.

6. On the day that your tenancy commences you will pay, in cleared funds (i.e. cash or banker's draft), the following sums of money:

	£
First period of rent in advance	400
Security Deposit	800
Total	1,200

Enclosed is a sample copy of the tenancy agreement for your information and an Application Form for you to complete, sign and return.

Please do not hesitate to contact me should you have any queries regarding this matter.

Yours sincerely

Landlord: *A. Landlord*

1.10 LANDLORD'S CHECKLIST

Acceptance of application subject to reference letters given ☐

Application forms given ☐

Application forms received with bank reference authorisation ☐

Reference letters sent ☐

Gas safety check booked ☐

Inventory prepared ☐

Sufficient number of keys available ☐

References chased ☐

References received ☐

Confirmation of satisfactory references and appointment to
check in letter sent ☐

Gas Safety Certificate received ☐

Tenancy agreement drafted ☐

All money received in cleared funds ☐

Tenancy agreement signed by all parties ☐

Check-In and Signed Inventory completed with tenant/s ☐

Copy of Gas Certificate given to tenant/s ☐

Receipt given to tenant/s ☐

Standing Order Form completed by tenant/s ☐

Contact information given to tenant/s ☐

Welcome Letter given to tenant/s ☐

Keys given to tenant/s ☐

Gas/electricity meter readings taken ☐

Utility companies informed of new tenant/s (including Council Tax) ☐

1.11 CONFIRMATION OF SATISFACTORY REFERENCES AND APPOINTMENT TO CHECK IN

A. Landlord
76–89 Alscot Road, London SE1 2EA
020 7394 4040

A. Tenant
98 Newcastle Street, London W12 8EL

Date: *20 December 2006*

Dear *A. Tenant*

Re: *10 Alscot Road, London SE1 3EJ*

I am writing to advise you that the referencing procedure has been successfully completed in respect of your application for the above-named property and I am pleased to confirm that it is now possible to proceed with your tenancy.

In order to release the keys for the property it is necessary to make arrangements for you to sign your tenancy agreement and pay the remaining sums of money due.

I therefore suggest that we meet at the property on *1 January 2007* at *9am* in order to carry out the handover and check-in procedure.

Please could you confirm that this appointment is convenient as soon as possible.

Yours sincerely

Landlord: *A. Landlord*

1.12 TENANT'S RECEIPT

Date: _____

Received by: _____

Payment made by: _____

In respect of: ☐ Rent   ☐ Deposit   ☐ Other (explain) _____
_____

Property address: _____
_____
_____

Amount paid: _____

Amount in words: _____
_____

Method of payment: ☐ Cash   ☐ Personal cheque
                   ☐ Banker's draft   ☐ Other

Signed:_____

Date: _____

Witnessed by: _____

1.13 STANDING ORDER MANDATE

INSTRUCTION TO THE BANK MANAGER

Name: _____

Address:_____

_____

_____

Bank name: _____

Address:_____

_____

_____

Account number: _____

Sort code: _____

Amount to be debited in £s: _____

In words: _____

_____

I hereby instruct you to make payment for the sum of [*insert amount*] to reach the recipient's account on [*insert day of month*].

Money is to be sent from my account as detailed above starting on the [*insert first date*] and monthly thereafter until further notice to:

Account name: _____

Address:_____

_____

_____

Account No.: _____

Sort code: _____

Signed:_____

Date: _____

(**Note:** Payments may leave your account approximately three working days prior to the rent-due date in order to ensure that payments are received by the landlord.)

1.14 WELCOME LETTER

A. Landlord
76–89 Alscot Road, London SE1 2EA
020 7394 4040

A. Tenant
10 Alscot Road, London SE1 3EJ

Date: *1 January 2007*

Dear *A. Tenant*

Re: *10 Alscot Road, London SE1 3EJ*

I would like to take this opportunity to welcome you to your new home and hope that you are very happy here.

I will try to ensure that I am available to answer any queries that you may have during the term of your tenancy, so please do not hesitate to contact me if you have any questions.

For your assistance, I have enclosed with this letter a directory of useful telephone numbers, some information about the local area and any instruction manuals/warranties for appliances and devices in the property.

Good luck with your unpacking!

Yours sincerely

Landlord: *A. Landlord*

CHAPTER 2

Gaining access

During the course of a tenancy you may require access to your property for a number of reasons. You might have to carry out a repair, conduct a viewing with potential new tenants or you may just be visiting the property to carry out a routine quarterly inspection. Whatever the reason, you **must** give your tenant reasonable notice that you intend to enter.

Once you have handed over the keys to the property, the tenant has the right to enjoy his privacy and the 'covenant of quiet enjoyment', which means that not only should you respect his privacy but also that you mustn't do anything to affect adversely his occupancy of the property. It's essential therefore that any appointments to enter the property be made in writing and clearly detail the reason why access is needed, the date you want to gain entry and the time of day.

There will usually be a clause in the tenancy agreement that orders the tenant to allow access for various reasons, provided that he has been given the right notice. If, however, you or your contractor arrives at the property to carry out an appointment and the tenant refuses access, for whatever reason, you must obey. If you enter the property against the tenant's will, you are breaching your tenant's rights and you could face serious charges regardless of whether your tenant is in breach of the terms of the tenancy agreement.

This chapter shows how you can effectively correspond with your tenant to ensure that when you do want access to the property, your tenant has been informed in the right way.

Arranging a general visit

You will usually be required to give your tenant a minimum of 24 to 48 hours' notice before you can gain access to the property, although the more time you can give to your tenant to prepare for the visit the better.

Routine visits

It's a good idea that as a landlord you carry out routine visits to the property in order to keep an eye on your investment and to give your tenant the opportunity to see you taking an interest in his well-being. A professional managing agent will usually visit a landlord's property on a quarterly basis and it's reasonable for you too to visit as frequently. Send your tenant a **ROUTINE VISIT (2.1)** letter when you want to do this and try to give him the opportunity to meet you at the property so that you can discuss any matters of concern with him.

Carrying out regular routine visits is the ideal way to keep up to date with the condition of the property and how it's being looked after by the tenant. Reassure your tenant that you are not there just to check up on him (although this is partly the reason for the visit), but you are also visiting the property to make sure that the building is in good repair and to plan for any future work that you might have to budget for.

Whilst you are at the property you should record your findings in detail by using a **PROPERTY VISIT REPORT (2.2)**. This report, carried out quarterly, will give a clear statement of how the property is being looked after as well as providing you with historical evidence of agreements or plans that have been made for works to be carried out.

Tip

If, during a routine property visit, you find out that your tenant is doing something that you don't like, you should speak to your tenant and ask him to make the necessary arrangements to put it right. If you have made detailed notes in the Property Visit Report, this will support you if you need to take action against your tenant later.

Viewings

If your current tenant is vacating the property shortly, you will probably want to carry out viewings with potential new tenants in the last month of the agreement to try to relet the property. You should have a clause in the tenancy agreement that allows this. Let your current tenant know when you would like to conduct these viewings in writing, with as much notice as possible, to give your tenant an opportunity to tidy and prepare.

 POTENTIAL NEW TENANT VIEWING (2.3)

Contractors

It's likely that at some point in the tenancy you will need to instruct a contractor to carry out repairs or maintenance. When you're looking for a tradesperson, be aware that you are sending a stranger into your tenant's home so it's advisable for you to do everything you can to ensure that the chosen contractor is trustworthy and suitable for the job.

You should always ask a tradesperson for references and, as the landlord, you should also request that your chosen contractor sign an agreement with you that states the terms under which your instruction is given. By having an agreement from each of your chosen contractors you are protecting the quality of the workmanship and standard of presentation as well as doing as much as you can to give the tenant peace of mind and security. A contractor who is unwilling to agree to your terms should be avoided.

 MAINTENANCE CONTRACTOR AGREEMENT (2.4)

TOP TIPS:

- Only use responsible contractors whom you have referenced and who are trustworthy.

- If you have never used a contractor before, try to be there with him on the first occasion.

- If you give the keys to a contractor and something goes wrong, your tenant will look to you to put things right.

- If your chosen contractor doesn't appear to be getting the job done in good time, see if you can get it done more efficiently elsewhere.

- If you always choose the lowest-priced contractor, you may find yourself with poor workmanship and the job could take twice as long to complete.

Don't forget...

| Poor workmanship and overlong timescales | = | Unhappy tenants | = | Headaches for landlords |

Access for maintenance/repairs

You should be holding spare keys to the tenant's property and if you know your chosen contractor well **and** you have the tenant's permission to do so, you might be happy to give him a set for access.

If a repair is required and the contractor has a set of keys, you should send a letter to your tenant advising when the appointment is due to take place and detail the repair to be carried out. It's important that you try to discuss the contractor's visit with the tenant in advance and make sure that he is happy for access to take place in his absence. When writing to the tenant you should give as much notice as possible.

 MAINTENANCE CONTRACTOR VISIT WITH KEYS (2.5)

If you're not holding a set of keys or you're unable to get a key to your chosen contractor, you can ask your tenant to be present at the appointment. Some tenants like to be at home during visits for their own peace of mind and some tenants work difficult hours so it's important to be as accommodating as possible in order to get the appointment confirmed. You may also find that some contractors are not happy to go into the property without someone being present. If the contractor doesn't have a set of keys, you should send a letter to your tenant asking him to confirm that the appointment you have suggested is convenient and offering him an opportunity to make alternative suggestions if it's not.

 MAINTENANCE CONTRACTOR VISIT WITHOUT KEYS (2.6)

Sometimes your contractor will visit the property and be unable to complete the works as instructed. He may need to order parts or the repair might be more complicated than originally believed. In these circumstances it's important to let your tenant know this information to keep him up to date with the progress of the repair and to give him the opportunity to make any necessary arrangements caused by the delay.

 CONTRACTOR UNABLE TO COMPLETE REPAIR (2.7)

Note

Many landlord and tenant disputes arise when tenants think their landlords are not carrying out maintenance to the property in accordance with the Housing Act and the terms of the tenancy agreement. By informing your tenant each step of the way with progress reports you will help assure your tenants that you care about the work that needs to be completed and that you want them to feel comfortable.

Gas safety inspections

All landlords must, in accordance with the Gas Safety (Installation and Use) Regulations 1998, ensure that their property has an up-to-date Landlord's Gas Safety Certificate where the property has gas appliances or installations.

Failure to hold a current certificate could jeopardise the life of your tenant and could lead to prosecution with penalties of imprisonment or fines of up to £5,000.

It's therefore essential that you know when your Landlord's Gas Safety Certificate is due to expire and that a new safety inspection is booked with a Corgi-registered engineer as soon as possible.

Don't wait until the current certificate expires before the next inspection takes place. Ensure that your next inspection is done approximately two weeks beforehand. This way, if there are any repairs needed, you can have them carried out prior to the expiration of your current certificate and you can make sure that your property and tenant are safe.

Your chosen Corgi-registered gas safety engineer may or may not have keys to the property so you should send your letters of appointment to your tenant depending on the circumstances. If your contractor has keys to the property, don't forget to try to discuss the visit with the tenant in advance to agree access arrangements and give the tenant plenty of notice when informing him of a visit.

 GAS SAFETY INSPECTION WITH KEYS (2.8)

 GAS SAFETY INSPECTION WITHOUT KEYS (2.9)

Both letters explain to the tenant the reason why the work is being carried out and confirm the date and time the contractor intends to carry out the inspection.

Another good reason for booking your gas safety inspection early is that you may experience problems accessing the property. There may be a problem with your keys or your Corgi-registered engineer could find that he has an emergency to deal with elsewhere that day.

Alternatively, it's possible that your tenant hasn't granted access and is not co-operating with your contractor, who wants to get the inspection done.

If your tenant isn't allowing access or is refusing entry to the contractor, it's important to write to your tenant so that you can highlight the importance of the gas safety inspection in relation to his own safety and well-being. Send a letter explaining to your tenant the reason why it's so important that the work is carried out and ask the tenant to contact the engineer urgently to arrange a suitable appointment.

 GAS SAFETY INSPECTION NO ACCESS 1 (2.10)

If your tenant continues to refuse access to the Corgi engineer, send a second letter advising him of your intention to take the matter further to protect yourself and your tenant.

 GAS SAFETY INSPECTION NO ACCESS 2 (2.11)

Protect yourself

By corresponding with your tenant regularly and detailing the importance of a Landlord's Gas Safety Record you are doing all that you can to ensure that your property is safe. If your tenant continues to refuse access, you should consider his reasons for doing so and think very carefully about whether this particular tenant is suitable for you and your property.

Emergencies

Sometimes it might be necessary to access your tenant's property extremely quickly if there is an emergency situation such as a flood, fire or gas leak. In such circumstances you may not have the opportunity to contact your tenant to let him know that you or a contractor needs to get into the property. You are entitled to enter the property under such conditions, and you should write to your tenant informing him why you entered the property and if there is any other information he should be advised of as a result of the emergency.

 EMERGENCY ACCESS HAS TAKEN PLACE (2.12)

2.1 ROUTINE VISIT

A. Landlord
76–89 Alscot Road, London SE1 2EA
020 7394 4040

A. Tenant
10 Alscot Road, London SE1 3EJ

Date: *10 January 2007*

Dear *A. Tenant*

Re: *10 Alscot Road, London SE1 3EJ*

I am writing to advise you that I would like to visit the above property in order to carry out a routine inspection.

You may wish to be present during this visit, but should you have a prior commitment, I will use my keys to the property.

I have made an appointment for *17 January 2007* at *2pm*. If I do not hear from you within five working days from the date of this letter, I will assume that this is convenient.

Thank you for your co-operation in this matter.

Yours sincerely

Landlord: *A. Landlord*

2.2 PROPERTY VISIT REPORT

Property address: _____
_____

Date of visit: _____
Time of visit: _____
Name of tenant/s present: _____
_____
_____

General standard of cleanliness: _____
_____
_____

Condition of kitchen and white goods:_____
_____
_____

Condition of bathroom and fittings: _____
_____
_____

Condition of floor coverings and decor: _____
_____
_____

Condition of garden: _____
_____
_____

Condition of external elevations:_____
_____
_____

Any signs of malicious damage: _____
_____
_____

Any signs of breaches of tenancy:_____
_____
_____

2.2 PROPERTY VISIT REPORT (continued)

Areas showing signs of wear and tear: _____
_____
_____

Areas in need of repair: _____
_____
_____

Areas that may need attention in next six months: _____
_____
_____

Any issues or comments raised by tenant/s:_____
_____
_____

Summary and action to be taken: _____
_____
_____
_____
_____
_____
_____
_____

Signed: _____(landlord)

Date: _____

2.3 POTENTIAL NEW TENANT VIEWING

A. Landlord
76–89 Alscot Road, London SE1 2EA
020 7394 4040

A. Tenant
10 Alscot Road, London SE1 3EJ

Date: *24 January 2007*

Dear *A. Tenant*

Re: *10 Alscot Road, London SE1 3EJ*

As you will be aware, I am currently seeking new tenants for the above-named property and I am writing to advise you of a viewing that I would like to conduct.

An appointment has been made to visit your property on *31 January 2007* at *1pm*.

You may wish to be present during this visit. However, should you have a prior commitment I will use my keys to the property.

I trust that this is satisfactory. However, should you wish to discuss this matter, please do not hesitate to contact me.

Thank you for your co-operation in this matter.

Yours sincerely

Landlord: *A. Landlord*

2.4 MAINTENANCE CONTRACTOR AGREEMENT

This agreement is made between the Contractor known as:

A. Contractor
_____

And the Client known as:

A. Landlord
_____

The Contractor hereby agrees:

1. To carry out all works/duties as instructed to a standard expected of a contractor qualified in that profession.

2. To provide, where necessary, clear quotations and to await instructions to proceed before commencing any work.

3. Not to take instructions from anyone else but the Client or a party authorised in writing by the Client. If additional work is required or reported by a third party, to advise the Client immediately and seek approval before commencing work.

4. To set out any additional costs that may become due prior to the instruction to proceed with the work.

5. Any work carried out that has not been authorised will not be charged.

6. All quotations and final invoices will be priced fairly and in line with other local tradespersons.

7. To provide clear descriptive invoices with reports detailing the work carried out and the cost of materials and labour.

8. To accept payment of invoices within 30 days of submission.

9. To maintain a clean and presentable image when attending the site and where possible to dress in clothing that displays the company logo.

10. To ensure that when the job is complete or at the end of a day's work the site is cleared to a good standard.

11. To hold Public Liability Insurance at all times and to be able to supply proof copies of documentation upon request.

12. In the instances that work has been carried out to an unsatisfactory standard to return to the site and make good/repair and not to be paid until such work has been completed and within a reasonable timescale set by the Client.

13. If works are not completed within the timescale, to pay the charges incurred by the Client from instructing a different contractor to carry out the necessary work.

2.4 MAINTENANCE CONTRACTOR AGREEMENT (continued)

Signed: _____(Contractor)

Registered Name and Address: _____

_____

_____

_____

Tel: _____

Fax:_____

Email:_____

Website: _____

Company Number:_____

Date: _____

WITNESSED BY:

Name: _____

Profession:_____

Address:_____

_____

_____

Signed:_____

Date: _____

2.5 MAINTENANCE CONTRACTOR VISIT WITH KEYS

A. Landlord
76–89 Alscot Road, London SE1 2EA
020 7394 4040

A. Tenant
10 Alscot Road, London SE1 3EJ

Date: *28 January 2007*

Dear *A. Tenant*

Re: *10 Alscot Road, London SE1 3EJ*

I am writing to advise you that an appointment has been made for a contractor known as *A. Contractor* to visit the above-named property to carry out the following work:

Fix the boiler.

You may wish to be present during this visit. However, should you have a prior commitment, the contractor will use my keys to the property.

An appointment has been made for *3 February 2007* at *11am* and if I do not hear from you I will assume that this is convenient.

Thank you for your co-operation in this matter.

Yours sincerely

Landlord: *A. Landlord*

2.6 MAINTENANCE CONTRACTOR VISIT WITHOUT KEYS

A. Landlord
76–89 Alscot Road, London SE1 2EA
020 7394 4040

A. Tenant
10 Alscot Road, London SE1 3EJ

Date: *28 January 2007*

Dear *A. Tenant*

Re: *10 Alscot Road, London SE1 3EJ*

I am writing to advise you that an appointment has been made for a contractor known as *A. Contractor* to visit the above-named property to carry out the following work:

Fix the boiler.

An appointment has been made for *3 February 2007* at *11am* and in this instance the contractor requires you to be present at the property.

Please could you therefore contact me to confirm that the above is convenient or to make suitable alternative arrangements.

Thank you for your co-operation in this matter.

Yours sincerely

Landlord: *A. Landlord*

2.7 CONTRACTOR UNABLE TO COMPLETE REPAIR

A. Landlord
76–89 Alscot Road, London SE1 2EA
020 7394 4040

A. Tenant
10 Alscot Road, London SE1 3EJ

Date: *28 January 2007*

Dear *A. Tenant*

Re: *10 Alscot Road, London SE1 3EJ*

As you are aware an appointment was recently made for a contractor known as *A. Contractor* to visit the above-named property to carry out the following work:

Fix the boiler.

Unfortunately, the contractor was unable to complete the work due to the following reason:

He was called away to another emergency.

Another appointment has therefore been made for *14 February 2007* at *10am* and if I do not hear from you, I will assume this is convenient.

Thank you for your co-operation in this matter.

Yours sincerely

Landlord: *A. Landlord*

2.8 GAS SAFETY INSPECTION WITH KEYS

A. Landlord
76–89 Alscot Road, London SE1 2EA
020 7394 4040

A. Tenant
10 Alscot Road, London SE1 3EJ

Date: *28 January 2007*

Dear *A. Tenant*

Re: *10 Alscot Road, London SE1 3EJ*

As you will be aware, it is required by law to have the gas appliances tested annually, pursuant to the Gas Safety (Installation and Use) Regulations 1998.

I am therefore writing to advise you that an appointment has been made for a contractor known as *A. Contractor* to visit the above-named property to carry out the necessary inspection.

You may wish to be present during this visit. However, should you have a prior commitment the contractor will use my keys to the property.

An appointment has been made for *14 February 2007* at *10am* and if I do not hear from you within five working days from the date of this letter, I will assume that this is convenient.

Thank you for your co-operation in this matter.

Yours sincerely

Landlord: *A. Landlord*

2.9 GAS SAFETY INSPECTION WITHOUT KEYS

A. Landlord
76–89 Alscot Road, London SE1 2EA
020 7394 4040

A. Tenant
10 Alscot Road, London SE1 3EJ

Date: *28 January 2007*

Dear *A. Tenant*

Re: *10 Alscot Road, London SE1 3EJ*

As you will be aware, it is required by law to have the gas appliances tested annually, pursuant to the Gas Safety (Installation and Use) Regulations 1998.

I am therefore writing to advise you that an appointment has been made for a contractor known as *A. Contractor* to visit the above-named property to carry out the necessary inspection.

An appointment has been made for *14 February 2007* at *10am* and in this instance the contractor requires you to be present at the property.

Please could you therefore contact me to confirm that the above is convenient or to make suitable alternative arrangements.

Thank you for your co-operation in this matter.

Yours sincerely

Landlord: *A. Landlord*

2.10 GAS SAFETY INSPECTION NO ACCESS 1

A. Landlord
76–89 Alscot Road, London SE1 2EA
020 7394 4040

A. Tenant
10 Alscot Road, London SE1 3EJ

Date: *28 January 2007*

Dear *A. Tenant*

Re: *10 Alscot Road, London SE1 3EJ*

As you will be aware, it is required by law to have the gas appliances tested annually, pursuant to the Gas Safety (Installation and Use) Regulations 1998.

It has been brought to my attention, however, that despite several attempts by my contractor a mutually agreed appointment has still not been arranged.

It is of the utmost importance, for your own safety, that you telephone the contractor immediately on *020 7123 4567* so that arrangements can be made to ensure your gas appliances are safe.

If you do not make arrangements for the above to take place, I take this opportunity to advise you that you are putting your safety at risk and I will have no choice but to contact the local Health and Safety Executive's office informing it of the situation.

Thank you for your co-operation in this matter.

Yours sincerely

Landlord: *A. Landlord*

2.11 GAS SAFETY INSPECTION NO ACCESS 2

A. Landlord
76–89 Alscot Road, London SE1 2EA
020 7394 4040

A. Tenant
10 Alscot Road, London SE1 3EJ

Date: *17 February 2007*

Dear *A. Tenant*

Re: *10 Alscot Road, London SE1 3EJ*

Despite my previous letters and communications from contractors, I understand that you have failed to make any contact in order that a gas safety inspection may be carried out.

As you have chosen to ignore all previous correspondence, I feel that it is my duty to advise you that you are compromising not only your own safety but also that of the property.

It is imperative that you telephone the contractor on *020 7123 4567* immediately upon receipt of this letter so that arrangements can be made to ensure your gas appliances are safe.

I take this opportunity to advise you that if you fail to arrange the above appointment within three days of this letter, I will have no option but to contact the local Health and Safety Executive, which could affect your supply of gas to the property.

Thank you for your co-operation in this matter.

Yours sincerely

Landlord: *A. Landlord*

2.12 EMERGENCY ACCESS HAS TAKEN PLACE

A. Landlord
76–89 Alscot Road, London SE1 2EA
020 7394 4040

A. Tenant
10 Alscot Road, London SE1 3EJ

Date: *17 February 2007*

Dear *A. Tenant*

Re: *10 Alscot Road, London SE1 3EJ*

I am writing to advise you that on *14 February 2007* at *7pm* emergency access was gained to your above-named property for the following reason:

There was a gas leak.

I apologise that it was not possible to inform you of the above; however, in the circumstances the situation presented a real risk to the property and it was necessary to resolve it as a matter of extreme urgency.

Please do not hesitate to contact me should you wish to discuss this matter further.

Yours sincerely

Landlord: *A. Landlord*

CHAPTER 3

Rent arrears

We would all like to dream that our tenants are perfect and will pay their rent in full and on time every month, but this is not always the case and sometimes your tenant may present you with the problem of rent arrears.

Stay calm!

Arrears can be stressful for all involved and sometimes you might feel like bashing down the door and screaming for your money, but this is **not** the way to deal with rent arrears as you are likely to find yourself facing harassment claims by your tenant!

By following some simple correspondence guidelines you will ensure that you have done everything you can to recover rent owed by your tenant **legally** and remain the professional landlord.

Keeping track

From the first day your tenant moves into the property make sure that you keep a record of payments that are due and when they are paid. This document will clearly show you any arrears and can be sent to tenants and guarantors to show why you are claiming outstanding rent. This is particularly helpful if you have more than one tenant in the property as it will enable your tenants to see who hasn't paid. If the tenants are held on a joint tenancy agreement, however, you should make it clear that they must all be equally responsible for the arrears and clear the debt as a single unit. Also, if you decide to make an application for possession against the tenant based on rent arrears, you will be required to provide a copy of the rent payment transactions under court rules.

 TENANT'S TRANSACTIONS (3.1)

The arrears procedure

So it's rent-due time and your tenant hasn't paid. What are you going to do?

Day 1

It's a good idea to give your tenant a polite telephone call to let him know that you haven't received your money. There may have been a problem with your tenant's bank and a quick phone call could resolve the matter immediately.

Day 7

If you don't get anywhere with your telephone call and the rent is seven days' overdue, send your tenant an official demand letter by first-class mail or hand deliver it.

 RENT DEMAND 1 (3.2)

Day 14

If, 14 days after the date that the rent is due, you haven't received the money from your tenant, you need to send another letter informing your tenant that if he doesn't pay, you may take the matter further and you may seek to recover possession of your property with costs.

 RENT DEMAND 2 (3.3)

If your tenant has provided you with a guarantor, now is a good time to send him a letter advising him that the tenant has not paid you rent according to his tenancy agreement. Normally the arrears will be paid quickly after this letter.

 GUARANTOR RENT DEMAND 1 (3.4)

Day 21

If, after 21 days, you haven't received any rent from your tenant, you should send another letter to him. This should be the final step before you consider taking further action to reclaim possession of your property.

 RENT DEMAND 3 (3.5)

If you previously sent a guarantor letter, you should now send another letter to inform the guarantor that you haven't received any rent despite trying to recover the amount owed from both parties. It will also confirm your intention to take legal action against him if the rent isn't paid.

 GUARANTOR RENT DEMAND 2 (3.6)

> **Note**
>
> If, in your letter, you don't include your name and an address in England or Wales where your tenant can serve notice or make payment of the rent, it doesn't constitute an official rent demand and could be thrown out by a judge if you need to go to court to evict your tenant for rent arrears!

Two months overdue

Now that your tenant has gone a whole month without paying rent and another month has become due, you can consider your tenant to be two months in arrears. This means that you have rights under the Housing Act to take action to reclaim possession of your property for breach of tenancy, and serving a Section 8 Notice will inform your tenant that you intend to take him to court if he doesn't pay within a further 14 days. The Notice **must** be in the prescribed form to be valid.

Next steps

If your tenant doesn't respond to your demands for rent, you are entitled to take legal action to seek possession of your property. You may also ask the court to make a judgment against your tenant for the arrears of rent and reasonable costs incurred. You can undertake this process yourself by obtaining the relevant forms from the local court, but it's essential that you be aware of the legal processes involved and that you have a sound understanding of what is required as mistakes can result in delays and loss of rent. It's a good idea to get some professional legal advice beforehand from a qualified solicitor who deals with landlord and tenant law or, alternatively, you may decide to instruct a solicitor to act on your behalf.

Protect yourself

Tenants who don't pay rent can pose a real threat to the security of your investment. Reclaiming arrears and possession through the small claims court can take time and could cost you money if you have monthly outgoings that need to be paid.

When a tenant falls seriously in arrears, there is no guarantee that you will recover the debt, particularly if the tenant's circumstances have changed dramatically or if he decides to leave the property without telling you where he has gone.

Some insurance companies supply cover to landlords which will protect you if your tenant doesn't pay the rent. For a small monthly premium you can ensure that your rent and any costs of evicting your problem tenant are taken care of, giving you peace of mind that your investment is not harmed financially.

3.1 TENANT'S TRANSACTIONS

Property address: _____

_____

_____

Tenant/s: _____

_____

_____

Date	Description	Debit	Credit	Balance
01.01.07	Rent 01.01.07 – 31.01.07	500.00		-500.00
01.01.07	S/O Payment Smith		250.00	-250.00
01.01.07	S/O Payment Johnson		250.00	0.00
01.02.07	Rent 01.02.07 – 28.02.07	500.00		-500.00
01.02.07	S/O Payment Smith		250.00	-250.00
01.03.07	Rent 01.03.07 – 31.03.07	500.00		-750.00

3.2 RENT DEMAND 1

A. Landlord
76–89 Alscot Road, London SE1 2EA
020 7394 4040

A. Tenant
10 Alscot Road, London SE1 3EJ

Date: *8 February 2007*

Dear *A. Tenant*

Re: *10 Alscot Road, London SE1 3EJ*

FORMAL DEMAND FOR OVERDUE RENT

I am writing to advise you that it appears from my records that your rent is currently overdue as follows:

OUTSTANDING RENT: £*500*   DUE: *1 February 2007*

I therefore kindly request that the outstanding balance be paid immediately and that you ensure that all future rental payments be made in full on the due date.

I take this opportunity to advise you that unpaid arrears could result in court action being taken against you for which you may become liable for legal costs.

If you would like to discuss this matter, please contact me urgently.

Thank you for your co-operation in this matter.

Yours sincerely

Landlord: *A. Landlord*

Address for Service: *76–89 Alscot Road, London SE1 2EA*

[**Note:** Your address must be in England or Wales.]

3.3 RENT DEMAND 2

A. Landlord
76–89 Alscot Road, London SE1 2EA
020 7394 4040

A. Tenant
10 Alscot Road, London SE1 3EJ

Date: *15 February 2007*

Dear *A. Tenant*

Re: *10 Alscot Road, London SE1 3EJ*

FORMAL DEMAND FOR OVERDUE RENT

I am writing to advise you that despite my previous reminder regarding outstanding rent, payment has not been made by you.

The current overdue amount is as follows:

OUTSTANDING RENT: £*500*   DUE: *1 February 2007*

I kindly request that, in order to avoid legal action being taken against you, the outstanding balance be paid immediately and that you ensure that all future rental payments are made in full and on the due date.

I take this opportunity to advise you that if you don't clear the arrears, I will consider making an application to the courts for possession of the property for which you may become liable for legal costs.

Please make your remittance by return.

Yours sincerely

Landlord: *A. Landlord*

Address for Service: *76–89 Alscot Road, London SE1 2EA*

[**Note:** Your address must be in England or Wales.]

3.4 GUARANTOR RENT DEMAND 1

A. Landlord
76–89 Alscot Road, London SE1 2EA
020 7394 4040

A. Guarantor
25 Norwich Lane, London SW17 2AP

Date: *20 February 2007*

Dear *A. Guarantor*

Re: *10 Alscot Road, London SE1 3EJ*

FORMAL DEMAND FOR OVERDUE RENT

I am writing to advise you that the tenant of the above-named property, for which you act as guarantor, currently has the following rent arrears:

OUTSTANDING RENT: £500   DUE: *1 February 2007*

I must therefore request, in accordance with your agreement, that either you or the tenant make payment of the above balance immediately.

I take this opportunity to advise you that unpaid arrears could result in court action being taken against both you and the tenant for which you may become liable for legal costs.

If you would like to discuss this matter, please do not hesitate to contact me urgently.

Thank you for your co-operation in this matter.

Yours sincerely

Landlord: *A. Landlord*

Address for Service: *76–89 Alscot Road, London SE1 2EA*

[**Note**: Your address must be in England or Wales.]

3.5 RENT DEMAND 3

A. Landlord
76–89 Alscot Road, London SE1 2EA
020 7394 4040

A. Tenant
10 Alscot Road, London SE1 3EJ

Date: *22 February 2007*

Dear *A. Tenant*

Re: *10 Alscot Road, London SE1 3EJ*

FORMAL DEMAND FOR OVERDUE RENT

OUTSTANDING RENT: £*500*   DUE: *1 February 2007*

I regret to note that you have not responded to the recent reminders regarding outstanding rent.

I therefore take this opportunity to advise you that it is my intention to take further action against you to regain possession of the property and to recover the outstanding arrears owed by you plus any legal costs that may be incurred.

If a County Court Judgment is entered against you for rent, this could affect your credit rating.

You may stop the above action by making remittance in full by return.

Yours sincerely

Landlord: *A. Landlord*

Address for Service: *76–89 Alscot Road, London SE1 2EA*

[**Note**: Your address must be in England or Wales.]

3.6 GUARANTOR RENT DEMAND 2

A. Landlord
76–89 Alscot Road, London SE1 2EA
020 7394 4040

A. Guarantor
25 Norwich Lane, London SW17 2AP

Date: *27 February 2007*

Dear *A. Guarantor*

Re: *10 Alscot Road, London SE1 3EJ*

FORMAL DEMAND FOR OVERDUE RENT

OUTSTANDING RENT: *£500*   DUE: *1 February 2007*

I regret to note that you have not responded to the recent reminder regarding outstanding rent in respect of the above-named property for which you act as guarantor to the tenant.

I therefore take this opportunity to advise you that it is my intention to take further action against you to regain possession of the property and to recover the outstanding arrears plus any legal costs that may be incurred.

If a County Court Judgment is entered against you for rent, this could affect your credit rating.

You may stop the above by making remittance in full by return.

Yours sincerely

Landlord: *A. Landlord*

Address for Service: *76–89 Alscot Road, London SE1 2EA*

[**Note**: Your address must be in England or Wales.]

CHAPTER 4

Responding to your tenant's requests

It's not uncommon for a tenant to ask to do something to or in the property which may make you question whether you are happy to agree.

When your tenant makes such a request there are four main points you should consider first of all:

1. Will the request cost you money?

2. Will the request cause damage to the property?

3. Is the tenant capable of fulfilling the request responsibly?

4. Will the request make it difficult for you to relet the property?

Of course, depending on what your answers are to these points, you may have already decided to either agree or disagree with the tenant's request, but do note that you cannot refuse your tenant's request unless you have a genuine and fair reason to refuse permission. For example, you cannot refuse permission simply because you don't like the tenant and want to be obstructive. Should this be the case, your refusal could be considered legally void.

The most common requests made by a tenant are to decorate the property, install satellite or cable television and to keep a pet. A tenant may also ask your permission to change some or all of the locks.

Decorating

If your tenant asks to decorate the property, at his own expense, consider the following points:

- You are giving him responsibility to oversee works to the property which will have a long-term impact on your investment.

- The job may be carried out badly and take time and effort to be put right.

- You may have to instruct a professional to put right any problems that may arise and you will have to try to claim back any damages from your tenant.

- More often than not the tenant will do the work himself, whether he is a proficient decorator or not, and this can lead to mistakes which hiring a tradesperson would have avoided.

However:

- Your property could end up looking a lot better than it does now and cost you very little or nothing.

- Your tenant is more likely to stay longer in a property that he has customised to his own taste.

- Your tenant will have a sense of pride in the property and treat it as a home rather than a short-term rental.

- Your tenant will sense that there is an element of trust and respect between you and this will improve your relationship as tenant and landlord.

If your tenant does request to carry out some decorating at the property and you are willing to consider it, you need to know what colour the tenant intends to use and where he wants to decorate.

 DECORATING – CONDITIONS FOR ACCEPTANCE (4.1)

It's important to ensure that you clarify your conditions in writing and that you make sure the tenant does the same. Whatever is agreed between you from this point will form the basis of any claim you might want to make later if the work isn't satisfactory.

If the tenant provides you with a satisfactory description of the work involved, including the location and the colour, you should set out, in a letter, the final conditions in which you are happy for the work to proceed. This will show the tenant exactly what you expect of him and confirms what will happen if any problems or damage occur as a result of the work.

 DECORATING – ACCEPTANCE (4.2)

Tip

If you are happy for your tenant to decorate your property, try to be involved in the process as much as possible. Arrange to meet the tenant at regular intervals to inspect the work and where possible offer advice and/or provide some of the materials to make sure that the work is completed to a good standard.

'If it ain't broke…!'

If your property is presented in a good decorative standard, there should be no reason for any redecorating to take place. Consider the possible effects of changing the appearance of your investment to suit the current tenant and how this could cause you problems when you want to relet the property.

Scenario

A tenant makes a special request to decorate one of the bedrooms in pink for the arrival of a new baby. Although the property is in generally good decorative order, the landlord agrees and some months later a baby girl is born and the room is ready in bright pink with a border to match. The tenant, however, begins to find it a struggle to support both the baby and the rent for the property and decides that when the tenancy expires she will move back to her parents' house. The landlord is left with a property that is difficult to rent to anyone except those with a baby girl (or a love for the colour pink) and has to pay out to have the room decorated to match the rest of the property again.

The above example is fictitious. However, many tenants will request to decorate rooms in different colours and you should be aware that this can make your property difficult to relet on the open market and could cause you financial loss.

Tip

Try suggesting alternatives to your tenant instead of decorating, such as changing curtains and lampshades, where a certain effect in a room is desired.

If you're not prepared for decorating work to go ahead, it's very important that you inform the tenant in writing of this with a valid reason so that should the tenant decide to take matters into his own hands and do it anyway, you have a record of non-acceptance that will help you should you need to make a claim against the tenant at the end of the tenancy.

 DECORATING – NON-ACCEPTANCE (4.3)

Installing a satellite dish or cable television

In today's society, most people use, to varying degrees, modern technology, such as mobile phones, the internet and digital or satellite television, and in lots of cases tenants will look for a property that caters to their needs in this area.

Most newly built properties now come with connections for satellite television, cable and broadband internet as standard, so a tenant looking to rent your property may take into account how up to date you are and how flexible you will be in allowing connections to these services.

It could certainly be a selling point if your tenant has the option of utilising such services in a rented property, and the work involved in putting these in place is usually minimal and doesn't cause any considerable damage to the property itself apart from a few drilled holes for cabling.

The risks involved in agreeing to have services such as satellite television and cable fitted are relatively low and could be beneficial when you come to relet the property. In order to ensure, however, that your tenant is made aware of the conditions for the work to proceed, you should send correspondence that confirms what is expected of the tenant and what will happen if problems do occur.

 INSTALLING SATELLITE TELEVISION OR CABLE – ACCEPTANCE (4.4)

Note

When a tenant asks permission to have satellite or cable television connected at the property you may be asked to sign a waiver agreement provided by the installer, which is a document confirming your consent for the work to take place and for your tenant to deal with the contractor directly. Check this agreement thoroughly and if you are in doubt about where responsibilities lie if problems do occur, contact the installer and clarify who carries the relevant liability.

Head lease and covenants

In some cases, depending on the type of property that you have and its location, you will have covenants that don't permit any changes to be made to the exterior of the building. If your property is in an apartment block or a conservation area, you should check immediately on your head lease and/or with the environmental health department of your local authority to see if fitting a satellite dish or drilling into the property is permitted. If you are unable to agree to a satellite dish or cable television being installed at the property, you should advise your tenant in writing and include the reason for your decision.

 INSTALLING SATELLITE TELEVISION OR CABLE – NON-ACCEPTANCE (4.5)

Note

If you give permission for your tenant to make changes to the outside of the property and you later find that your lease or local authority forbids such work, you will be responsible for removing any equipment and/or ensuring the work is made good to the exterior. Your tenant may also make a financial claim against you if he has a subscription that he is no longer able to maintain because of the removal of hardware, etc.

Tip

If your rented property has a head lease, which may affect your tenant, you must provide a copy of this document at the start of the tenancy. Alternatively, make sure that your tenancy agreement clearly states clauses in the head lease that are relevant to the tenant's occupancy.

Pets

Whilst keeping a pet might make your tenant feel more at home in your property, you shouldn't forget the risks involved in agreeing to this request and the likely outcomes that will affect your investment. There are two main areas of concern when considering whether to allow a tenant to keep a pet:

1. How much will the pet contribute to the overall natural wear and tear to the property?

2. How much damage could be caused to the property if the tenant doesn't look after the pet responsibly?

The type of pet your tenant is asking to keep is extremely important when determining the above points.

If your tenant is asking to keep a goldfish at the property, the risks are considerably small. If the fish isn't fed, it will die in the tank; a fish doesn't catch and spread fleas. In fact, one of the only real risks is that the tank may fall and smash to the floor, and even this is unlikely to cause serious damage.

The most common types of household pets (except goldfish), such as cats, dogs, birds, rabbits and rodents, are the ones that can seriously affect the condition of your property and these are the pets your tenant is most likely to request permission to keep.

The problems associated with pets

- **Fleas**

  Must be removed by a process of fumigation which should be carried out by a professional to ensure all areas are covered.

- **Damage to furnishings caused by scratching or chewing**

  Over a period of time, this will make your property appear worn and difficult to relet.

- **Unpleasant smells**

  Can be difficult to remove and may require professional cleaning and fumigation.

- **Unsociable levels of noise**

  Complaints can strain relationships between landlords and neighbours.

- **Damage caused to gardens by digging or covering up faeces**

  Can be expensive to remedy.

Unless you're prepared to take these risks and you're happy to work closely with your tenant towards the end of the agreement to put any problems right or make a claim against his deposit, you shouldn't agree to the request.

> **Note**
>
> Many landlords stipulate in the advertising of their property, 'No Pets, No Smokers, No Children'. They do this because they know that by allowing any of the above they are accepting that the natural wear and tear to the property will be increased over a shorter period of time. You may be unable to make claims against your tenant for anything except malicious damage caused by the pet or the keeping of the animal if you consent to pets.

If you're prepared to take the risks associated with pets in rented property and you're willing to give consent to your tenant, it's important to confirm your acceptance and to try to protect yourself as much as possible by informing the tenant of the terms of your agreement.

 PETS – ACCEPTANCE (4.6)

If, however, you don't wish for your tenant to keep a pet at the property, you should advise him accordingly in writing, giving your reasons.

 PETS – NON-ACCEPTANCE (4.7)

Changing the locks

Some tenants will ask for permission to change the locks at the property and you should find out specifically why your tenant has made this request before agreement is given.

If the tenant has lost his keys, this can present a serious risk to the security of the property and affects both you and the tenant. If the keys cannot be found, it's reasonable to consider changing the locks to the property to ensure continued safety. Your tenant should be responsible for the cost of this.

If the tenant is applying for an insurance policy, he may be required to fit certain types of lock to the property in order to comply with the terms of his policy. This is common practice with some insurance agencies and is also a fair reason for making the request, although you should consider the extent of the changes the tenant wishes to make.

Where you are in agreement with your tenant changing the locks, you should confirm in writing the terms under which you are happy for the work to proceed.

 CHANGING LOCKS – ACCEPTANCE (4.8)

If you're not happy for the locks to be changed by the tenant, you should inform him in writing advising him of the reasons why.

 CHANGING LOCKS – NON-ACCEPTANCE (4.9)

Don't forget...

Maintaining the security of your property is very important and you should, as landlord, make sure that you have fulfilled your obligations to repair any locks that are faulty or in poor condition. Renting a property which isn't secure could lead to burglary and damage to both parties' possessions, and claims for insurance may be rejected if the property isn't secure, plus you may be liable for any losses the tenant may suffer as a result of any delay in dealing with it.

Tip

Sometimes tenants will cut extra sets of keys which they may forget to tell you about and they might not surrender them at the termination of the tenancy. An inexpensive way for you to maintain security is to change the locks on the main entrance door at the end of each tenancy and always make sure that you hold a full set of spare keys to the property.

4.1 DECORATING – CONDITIONS FOR ACCEPTANCE

A. Landlord
76–89 Alscot Road, London SE1 2EA
020 7394 4040

A. Tenant
10 Alscot Road, London SE1 3EJ

Date: *1 March 2007*

Dear *A. Tenant*

Re: *10 Alscot Road, London SE1 3EJ*

Further to your request to carry out some decorating works at the above-named property, I am writing to advise you that in order to give consent for you to proceed you must provide the following:

1. A colour sample/fabric swatch

2. A diagram of all areas that you wish to decorate

Upon receipt of the above, I will consider your request and advise you in writing of the decision.

I trust this is satisfactory.

Yours sincerely

Landlord: *A. Landlord*

4.2 DECORATING – ACCEPTANCE

A. Landlord
76–89 Alscot Road, London SE1 2EA
020 7394 4040

A. Tenant
10 Alscot Road, London SE1 3EJ

Date: *1 March 2007*

Dear *A. Tenant*

Re: *10 Alscot Road, London SE1 3EJ*

Further to your request to carry out some decorating works at the above-named property, I am writing to confirm that the colour sample that you have provided is satisfactory and I am in agreement with the areas that you wish to decorate. You may therefore proceed on the following basis:

- All work carried out by you must be to a high standard and you will take all responsibility for poor workmanship or damage caused by the work.

- All work surfaces will be prepared properly and suitable materials will be used to protect the property from damage.

- All equipment used in connection with the works will be provided by you and will be suitable for the job.

- I will not be held responsible for any loss or personal injury caused as a result of these works.

- I reserve the right to withdraw consent at any time and to hire contracted tradespersons to complete the works if the standard is unsatisfactory.

- You will pay all costs associated with the works including, if applicable, any repair or redecorating work that may be required in accordance with the above.

I trust this is satisfactory. However, please do not hesitate to contact me should you wish to discuss this matter further.

Yours sincerely

Landlord: *A. Landlord*

4.3 DECORATING – NON-ACCEPTANCE

A. Landlord
76–89 Alscot Road, London SE1 2EA
020 7394 4040

A. Tenant
10 Alscot Road, London SE1 3EJ

Date: *1 March 2007*

Dear *A. Tenant*

Re: *10 Alscot Road, London SE1 3EJ*

Further to your request to carry out some decorating work at the above-named property, I am writing to advise you that I regretfully cannot give my consent at this time for the following reason:

The property was recently redecorated, so I do not believe that further refurbishment is needed at this time.

Thank you for your co-operation in this matter.

Yours sincerely

Landlord: *A. Landlord*

4.4 INSTALLING SATELLITE TELEVISION OR CABLE – ACCEPTANCE

A. Landlord
76–89 Alscot Road, London SE1 2EA
020 7394 4040

A. Tenant
10 Alscot Road, London SE1 3EJ

Date: *1 March 2007*

Dear *A. Tenant*

Re: *10 Alscot Road, London SE1 3EJ*

Further to your request to have satellite television connected at the above-named property, I am writing to confirm that this is acceptable. You may therefore proceed on the following basis:

- All work carried out to install the system must be to a high standard and you will take all responsibility for poor workmanship or damage caused by the work.

- All internal and external work surfaces will be protected from damage.

- The contractor that you use for installation will be a professional tradesperson registered with an official body or employed directly by the service provider.

- I will not be held responsible for any loss or personal injury caused by or as a result of these works.

- You will pay all costs associated with the works including, if applicable, any repair or redecorating work that may be required in accordance with the above.

- You will pay for and maintain the system and any relevant servicing or repairs during the term of your tenancy.

- When you vacate the property, you will ensure that any items associated with the installation, such as satellite dishes and/or components, are professionally removed and all drilled holes are filled and decorated to match the existing decoration.

Please do not hesitate to contact me should you wish to discuss this matter further.

Yours sincerely

Landlord: *A. Landlord*

4.5 INSTALLING SATELLITE TELEVISION OR CABLE – NON-ACCEPTANCE

A. Landlord
76–89 Alscot Road, London SE1 2EA
020 7394 4040

A. Tenant
10 Alscot Road, London SE1 3EJ

Date: *1 March 2007*

Dear *A. Tenant*

Re: *10 Alscot Road, London SE1 3EJ*

Further to your request to have satellite television connected at the above-named property, I am writing to advise you that I regretfully cannot give my consent at this time for the following reason:

Local residents have raised concern over the appearance of satellite dishes on the outside of houses in the local area and in this instance I have agreed that dishes are unsightly and have a detrimental effect on the appearance of this property.

Also, satellite dishes are not permitted under the terms of the head lease.*

Thank you for your co-operation in this matter.

Yours sincerely

Landlord: *A. Landlord*

[* Delete if appropriate.]

4.6 PETS – ACCEPTANCE

A. Landlord
76–89 Alscot Road, London SE1 2EA
020 7394 4040

A. Tenant
10 Alscot Road, London SE1 3EJ

Date: *1 March 2007*

Dear *A. Tenant*

Re: *10 Alscot Road, London SE1 3EJ*

Further to your request to keep a *cat* at the above-named property, I am writing to confirm that this is acceptable. You may therefore proceed on the following basis:

- You are responsible for any damage caused by or as a result of keeping a pet at the property including, where applicable, the garden area.

- Where relevant, you will provide and keep the pet in suitable accommodation designed for the purpose.

- You will be responsible for any costs associated with the increased wear and tear to the property caused by keeping a pet.

- You will not allow the pet to disturb neighbours or to cause unsociable levels of noise at the property.

- When you vacate the property, you will instruct and pay for professional cleaning tradespersons to clean and deflea the premises and to steam clean the carpets. You will be asked to provide the details of the contractors that you use and a breakdown of the work carried out must be made available.

- I will not be held responsible for any loss or personal injury caused by or as a result of keeping a pet at the property.

I trust this is satisfactory. However, please do not hesitate to contact me should you wish to discuss this matter further.

Yours sincerely

Landlord: *A. Landlord*

4.7 PETS – NON-ACCEPTANCE

A. Landlord
76–89 Alscot Road, London SE1 2EA
020 7394 4040

A. Tenant
10 Alscot Road, London SE1 3EJ

Date: *1 March 2007*

Dear *A. Tenant*

Re: *10 Alscot Road, London SE1 3EJ*

Further to your request to keep a *cat* at the above-named property, I am writing to advise you that I regretfully cannot give my consent at this time for the following reason:

I do not want my decorations and furnishings to be harmed in any way.

Thank you for your co-operation in this matter.

Yours sincerely

Landlord: *A. Landlord*

4.8 CHANGING OR ADDING NEW LOCKS – ACCEPTANCE

A. Landlord
76–89 Alscot Road, London SE1 2EA
020 7394 4040

A. Tenant
10 Alscot Road, London SE1 3EJ

Date: *1 March 2007*

Dear *A. Tenant*

Re: *10 Alscot Road, London SE1 3EJ*

Further to your request to change the locks to the *front door* at the above-named property, I am writing to confirm that this is acceptable. You may therefore proceed on the following basis:

- All work carried out to change the locks must be to a high standard and you will take all responsibility for poor workmanship or damage caused by the work.
- All internal and external work surfaces will be protected from damage.
- The contractor that you use for installation will be a professional tradesperson and where possible will be registered with an official body.
- I will not be held responsible for any loss or personal injury caused by or as a result of these works.
- You will pay all costs associated with the works including, if applicable, any repair or redecorating work that may be required in accordance with the above.
- You will provide me with sets of any new keys immediately after the work has taken place.
- You will confirm the number of new keys that have been cut and return all sets to me at the end of the tenancy.

I trust this is satisfactory. However, please do not hesitate to contact me should you wish to discuss this matter further.

Yours sincerely

Landlord: *A. Landlord*

4.9 CHANGING OR ADDING NEW LOCKS – NON-ACCEPTANCE

A. Landlord
76–89 Alscot Road, London SE1 2EA
020 7394 4040

A. Tenant
10 Alscot Road, London SE1 3EJ

Date: *1 March 2007*

Dear *A. Tenant*

Re: *10 Alscot Road, London SE1 3EJ*

Further to your request to change the locks to the front door at the above-named property, I am writing to advise you that I regretfully cannot give my consent at this time for the following reason:

I am only willing to change the locks if my tenants have lost their keys, but as this is not the case in your circumstances, I do not wish the decoration of my front door to be disturbed in any way.

Thank you for your co-operation in this matter.

Yours sincerely

Landlord: *A. Landlord*

CHAPTER 5

Complaints and breach of tenancy

During your time as a landlord, at some point it's likely that one of your tenants will break a term of his tenancy agreement or cause someone to complain about him. Knowing how to deal with this situation professionally will help prevent arguments and ensure that, if further action is required, you have done everything you can to solve the situation reasonably.

Talk to your tenant

It's easy for tempers to flare when a tenant acts in a manner that gives you concern. Aggressive conflict will only make things worse. A combination of good social skills and the right communication techniques are what you need when a tenant is in breach of his agreement.

Speaking to your tenant face to face can be a daunting prospect for some landlords, but many situations can be resolved quickly and amicably by having a polite conversation where both parties have the opportunity to discuss the problem.

Effective verbal communication in this way can often give you a better understanding of why the situation has occurred and a clear idea of what the tenant is likely to do to remedy the matter.

Whatever the result of any conversation, it's important to document the results and to inform the tenant of what has been agreed in writing, so that both parties are aware of the situation and of any plans put in place that have been agreed to solve the problem. Make sure that you retain copies of any correspondence and keep records of conversations as you may need to rely on these later to show that you have acted reasonably should the matter escalate.

Note

Act quickly! When your tenant breaches a term of the tenancy agreement or you have received a complaint against your tenant, you should respond with urgency and efficiency. Continued breaches of a tenancy can lead to damage to your property, unhappy neighbours and costly or time-consuming court proceedings.

Noise complaints

The most common complaint made about tenants in rented accommodation is unsociable levels of noise.

Between the hours of 7pm and 7am it's reasonable to presume that your tenant won't cause a disturbance to the neighbours by loud music or noise coming from the property.

If your tenant is noisy, it's likely that the first you will hear of it is from one of the neighbours. If a neighbour has your contact details (which is a good idea), you will probably receive a phone call or letter informing you that your tenant has caused a disturbance due to excessive noise levels being created.

Tip

If you receive a noise complaint from a neighbour, try to find out all the details before you approach your tenant. You need to know what has caused the noise and when the situation occurred. You should also find out if your neighbour has approached the tenant directly and if so, what was said. In some cases, a neighbour asking your tenant politely to turn down his music or to reduce noise resolves the problem immediately.

If you have received a complaint against your tenant for unsociable levels of noise, you should send him a letter asking him to respect his neighbour's right to quiet enjoyment of the property and to ensure the noise levels don't exceed reasonable levels in the future.

 NOISE COMPLAINT 1 (5.1)

If the problem wasn't an isolated incident and you receive further complaints after you have corresponded with your tenant, you should write to him again referring to your previous letter. Advise your tenant that you will log the complaint with the Noise Nuisance/Environmental Health Department of your local authority and ask the complainant to keep a diary of any further disturbances. This will help you if you need to take the matter further or for a time in the future when you will be re-evaluating whether you want to relet the property to the same tenant.

 NOISE COMPLAINT 2 (5.2)

The police have limited powers when it comes to noise disturbance. However, if the problem persists and your tenant refuses to respect your requests to reduce the level of noise, you should write to your tenant again and report the matter to the local constabulary. With this letter you may also wish to include a Notice Requiring Possession of the property, which usually comes in the form of a Section 21 Notice, depending on the type of tenancy agreement you're using.

 NOISE COMPLAINT 3 (5.3)

By this stage it's also possible that the Noise Nuisance/Environmental Health Department will consider monitoring your property. If this is the case, you should discuss the matter further with them as they have the right to remove certain equipment that could be causing the disturbance.

> **Note**
>
> It's very difficult to evict a tenant on the basis of unsociable levels of noise. You will need to have a very detailed record of instances when the noise has occurred including copies of complaint letters from neighbours, correspondence which you have sent to the tenant and, most likely, reports from the local police and the relevant department of your local authority to back up your claim. It's sometimes quicker to serve a standard notice to terminate the tenancy at the next available

point if your tenant is continually causing disturbances due to unsociable levels of noise.

Note

If the disturbance is due to poor sound insulation in the property, you may be ordered to rectify this by your local Environmental Health Department under new powers under the Housing Act 2004 expected to come into force in April 2006. These are likely to change the previous situation where the landlord could not be required to improve sound insulation if the property met the existing building regulations standards at the time it was built or when it was converted into a flat.

Gardens

If a garden hasn't been maintained through the seasons, it can result in time-consuming and expensive work to bring it back to a reasonable standard.

If you want your tenant to be responsible for the maintenance and upkeep of the garden, you must make sure that there is a clause in the tenancy agreement stating this; otherwise, you will have no recourse against your tenant if the garden is left in poor condition at the end of the tenancy.

Where it's clearly stated in the agreement that your tenant is responsible for the garden, you should make sure that each time you visit the property notes are made with regard to its current condition and that you inform your tenant when you notice that the garden needs some maintenance. It's a good idea to take photographs which you can refer to later should you need to prove that your tenant has failed to maintain the garden over a period of time.

 UNTIDY GARDEN (5.4)

Alternatively, you may consider employing a gardener to look after the garden, the cost to be included in the rent. If you do so, your tenancy agreement must provide for access by the gardener.

Tip

Lots of tenants may not have any previous experience of looking after a garden and it's worth considering this when asking any tenant to maintain one at your property. You can help your tenant by ensuring that the garden is in a manageable condition at the start of the tenancy. You could also supply some basic gardening tools and maybe a guide to garden maintenance. If your tenant fails to maintain the garden after this, you have a good reason to make a claim against his deposit at the end of the tenancy.

Satellite dishes

Lots of tenants like to have the benefit of satellite or cable television and some will make arrangements to have these services installed without your consent.

If you don't want your tenant to fix a satellite dish to the exterior of the property, you must make sure that there is a clause in the tenancy agreement which covers this or you could find it difficult when enforcing its removal. See chapter 4 regarding head leases, covenants and environmental restrictions that may apply.

If you do have clauses in your tenancy agreement stating that your tenant is not permitted to have a satellite dish fixed to the exterior of the property, or there are restrictive covenants in place, you should inform the tenant in writing of his breach and demand the dish to be removed within a short period of time.

 UNAUTHORISED SATELLITE DISH (5.5)

Property damage

Damage caused to your property can seriously affect your investment in the long term and it can cost you a great deal of time and money to put it right.

Sometimes your tenant may not be aware that he is causing damage to the property through lack of experience or understanding of property maintenance. This is, however, no excuse, and if you recognise damage that is being caused as a result of your tenant's behaviour, you should take steps to resolve it immediately.

Exterior damage

Tenants often assume that they're not responsible for the areas that fall outside the property. Your tenancy agreement should contain clauses that place responsibility on the tenant to maintain certain areas of the exterior and to inform you of any external damage immediately. As landlord you have obligations to maintain and carry out repairs to the property, but there are instances where damage caused by the tenant's neglect should be taken care of at the tenant's expense.

Examples of exterior damage that can be caused by tenants include:

- Blocked gutters

- Broken windows or glass in greenhouses

- Overgrowing trees affecting boundaries or high cables

- Drilled holes in masonry for fixings

- Leaking car batteries left on driveways

If you recognise signs of damage caused by your tenant, you must advise him in writing of the details and request that the work be put right at the tenant's expense without delay. You should highlight that failure on your tenant's part to repair the problem could result in charges being made against his deposit at the end of the tenancy.

 DAMAGE TO EXTERNAL DECORATIONS (5.6)

Internal damage

When you carry out a routine visit to the property and you find that damage is being caused to the internal decoration or furniture and fittings because of neglectful or malicious behaviour on the part of your tenant, you must act quickly.

As discussed earlier, your tenant may not be aware that he is causing damage to the property, but this is no excuse and the responsibility should lie with the tenant to repair and make good the damage.

If your tenant is causing internal damage to the property, you must advise him in writing of the details and request that the work be put right at his own expense without delay.

 DAMAGE TO INTERNAL DECORATIONS (5.7)

> **Tip**
>
> When asking your tenant to effect a repair to the property after he has caused damage, consider offering assistance to locate a suitable tradesperson. You may have a contractor whom you use regularly for this kind of work and any involvement you can have to ensure the work is carried out by a qualified person will benefit the condition of your property at the end of the day.

Threatening or antisocial behaviour

Hopefully you will never experience a tenant whose actions appear threatening or aggressive. However, you may find an occasion when a complaint is made about your tenant for something that you consider to be unlawful, indecent or disruptive whilst living in the property.

Behaviour such as this may include:

- Causing nuisance or annoyance to neighbours

- Drug taking

- Prostitution

You should be very careful not to accuse your tenant of any unlawful act without sufficient proof. However, you should still correspond with your tenant to inform him that a serious complaint has been made regarding his behaviour.

 THREATENING/ANTISOCIAL BEHAVIOUR (5.8)

If you're unlucky enough to have an antisocial tenant, you should consider proceedings for eviction, and the relevant notices will need to be served as soon as possible.

Smoking

Allowing your tenant to smoke inside your property can cause long-term damage to the decoration (turning your walls yellow!) and you risk cigarette burns to floor carpets and furniture. Smoking in a furnished property will particularly increase the wear and tear of any fabric items on your inventory. Cigarette smells are difficult to remove in properties where tenants have smoked for a long period of time without sufficient ventilation and this can make it difficult to secure new tenants when it comes to reletting.

If there is a clause in the tenancy agreement which states that the tenant will not smoke inside the property and you discover that the tenant is in breach of this term, you should write to the tenant asking him to smoke outside and away from the property.

 SMOKING IN PROPERTY (5.9)

Pets

As discussed in chapter 4, pets can cause lots of problems for landlords if they are allowed to be kept at the property.

It's a good idea if you're not happy for your tenant to keep a pet that you include a clause in the tenancy agreement which details this. If a tenant hasn't been told that he cannot have a pet, he might assume that you don't mind and many tenants will use this argument when a landlord tries to take action against them to have the animal (or the tenants) removed… usually the tenant wins!

If your tenant is keeping a pet at the property and you would like him to remove it, you should write a letter asking him do so.

 UNAUTHORISED PET IN PROPERTY (5.10)

Note

Any tenancy agreement clause prohibiting pets must be properly drafted or it will be invalid.

Vehicles

When tenants move into a property many will have vehicles that they use for transportation and sometimes damage or complaint can be caused due to careless behaviour by your tenant and the use of his chosen vehicle.

Lack of proper maintenance and repair of vehicles can lead to leakages on driveways which can stain and damage your property. Corroded, rusty vehicle parts and old car batteries can also contaminate lawns and flowerbeds making it impossible for things to grow without considerable gardening work to put it right. If you recognise that your tenant's vehicle is in a poor state of repair and is causing damage to the external grounds of your property, you should write to him requesting the vehicle to be removed and that any repairs should be carried out at his expense.

 ### TENANT'S VEHICLE CAUSING DAMAGE TO EXTERNAL GROUNDS (5.11)

Vehicles that block other people's access routes or are parked in the wrong designated spaces can cause annoyance and inconvenience. More seriously, tenants will often park bicycles in communal areas or just inside a building's entranceway where there is no designated or specific bicycle locking point. This presents a serious risk of loss of life in the event of a fire, particularly if the bicycle is parked within the fire escape route of a block of apartments.

Obstructing access routes or fire escapes could lead to prosecution and, as a landlord, you have a responsibility to ensure that your tenant is made aware of the risks involved. Write to your tenant accordingly and be sure to follow up the letter to check that the vehicle has been removed.

 ### TENANT'S VEHICLE PARKED IN UNAUTHORISED AREA (5.12)

Alternatively, try to ensure that a designated area is available where your tenant can chain his bicycle securely, then he is less likely to block access ways.

If your property is located within an apartment block or your tenants are held on individual agreements with communal shared areas, post clear, bold fire safety notices in the entranceways and along fire escape routes informing the tenants that the areas must remain free of all vehicles and should not be blocked in any way.

Unauthorised occupiers

Only those named on the tenancy agreement (and, if appropriate, their immediate families, e.g. their spouses and children) should be living at the property and if you believe that your tenant has moved additional people into the property without your consent, you should take action immediately.

You shouldn't allow guests to become tenants without going through the proper referencing procedure. Your existing tenant could be subletting your property and taking valuable income from your pocket whilst increasing the wear and tear on your investment.

Occupiers who are not named on the tenancy agreement should undergo the necessary referencing procedure and if they are successful, they can then be named on the tenancy agreement. Occupiers who are not named on the tenancy agreement have no liability to uphold the terms of the contract and are less likely to care for the well-being of your property. In many cases, those who move into rented property without informing you will have previous issues that could stand in the way of them being considered for a property through the usual routes.

Make sure that the rent you receive is being paid by the named tenant on the tenancy agreement. Look out for any money that is being paid by somebody else as this is an indication that a person other than your legal tenant is living at the property without your written permission.

You should have a clause in the tenancy agreement which states that the tenant will not sublet the property or accept any additional paying or non-paying long-term guests, occupants or otherwise who may be considered to be living at the property.

If you suspect or have evidence that your tenant has moved additional occupants into the property without your consent, you should send him a letter which details why this is unacceptable and informs him of the necessary procedures. If you're not prepared to consider an additional applicant, you should make this clear to your tenant and check to make sure that the unauthorised tenant has vacated.

 UNAUTHORISED OCCUPANTS AT PROPERTY (5.13)

If the unauthorised occupier fails to vacate, your next step should be to serve a notice to terminate on the tenant, and then, if necessary, bring proceedings for possession.

Repairs

As landlord, you have obligations under the Housing Act 1985 to carry out any necessary repairs and maintenance to the property within reasonable timescales.

Your tenant, however, also has obligations to ensure that he informs you of a need for maintenance in a timely fashion in order to avoid continued and extensive damage, as well as carrying out and being responsible for the costs of any repairs where he has been at fault.

A good relationship between you and your contractor will ensure that when the contractor visits the property to carry out a repair he will advise you of the following:

- How long the problem has been going on
- If the tenant is at fault

If a tenant fails to notify you of a repair in good time and, as a result, the extent of the works required to put the fault right are dramatically increased, your tenant should be made liable for the extra cost incurred by you. You should send a letter informing the tenant of the situation along with a copy of the contractor's report and invoice and ask the tenant to send you payment for the amount claimed.

 FAILURE TO NOTIFY OF REPAIR – TENANT LIABLE (5.14)

Occasionally a tenant will inform you of a repair and your chosen contractor will advise you that the fault was caused by neglectful behaviour or misuse by the tenant. Examples of this might be:

- cutlery blocking the waste disposal unit;

- the tenant's washing machine connected incorrectly causing flooding;

- freezer seals split by de-icing with knives;

- blocked drains caused by grease and food residues.

If this is the case, your tenant should be held responsible for the cost of the repair and informed of his obligations to ensure that the faults caused by misuse or neglectful behaviour are dealt with at his own expense.

 REPAIR CARRIED OUT – TENANT LIABLE (5.15)

Tip

Pay your contractor! Even in the instance where your tenant is liable for the cost of a repair, you should still settle the contractor's invoice in full within the stated timescales and pursue your tenant directly for the money. You're likely to need the services of the contractor again and if you have caused problems with payment, he will be unlikely to do business with you in the future.

Don't forget...

Regardless of knowledge or experience your tenant is obliged to inform you of any repairs within good time to ensure that the property does not suffer extensive damage. Your tenant should be considered liable for the additional costs where he has failed in these responsibilities. **Ignorance is no excuse!**

Changing locks

As discussed in chapter 4, there are a few circumstances where you may need to change the locks and you should always be informed if your tenant intends to make any changes to the security of your property.

It's particularly important that you hold a full set of keys to the property and if you discover that you are unable to gain access to the property and suspect that your tenant has changed the locks, you should try to find out immediately why this work has taken place without your consent.

 TENANT HAS CHANGED LOCKS (5.16)

> **Note**
>
> The tenant may be justified in changing the locks if you have been using your keys to gain access to the property without the tenant's knowledge and/or consent, particularly if the tenant has expressly asked you not to enter the property without an agreed appointment. This is because you will have been in breach of the 'covenant of quiet enjoyment' in the tenancy agreement. Male landlords of female tenants living alone should be particularly careful to respect their wishes.

5.1 NOISE COMPLAINT 1

A. Landlord
76–89 Alscot Road, London SE1 2EA
020 7394 4040

A. Tenant
10 Alscot Road, London SE1 3EJ

Date: *1 March 2007*

Dear *A. Tenant*

Re: *10 Alscot Road, London SE1 3EJ*

I am writing to advise you that a complaint has been made against you in respect of:

Unsatisfactory levels of noise

The incident took place on *27 February 2007* at *1am*.

Whilst I appreciate that this may have been an isolated incident, I must request that noise be kept to a minimum and that peaceful enjoyment of both your property and your neighbours' be respected and maintained at all times.

Failure to comply with the above may constitute a breach of the terms of your tenancy agreement and repeated complaints regarding levels of noise may result in further action being taken against you, which could include repossession of the property.

Should further complaints be received in this matter I will have no hesitation in contacting the local council, which has the power to monitor unsociable noise levels and can, at their discretion, legally remove musical players and equipment from the property.

Please do not hesitate to contact me should you wish to discuss this matter further.

Thank you for your co-operation.

Yours sincerely

Landlord: *A. Landlord*

5.2 NOISE COMPLAINT 2

A. Landlord
76–89 Alscot Road, London SE1 2EA
020 7394 4040

A. Tenant
10 Alscot Road, London SE1 3EJ

Date: *1 April 2007*

Dear *A. Tenant*

Re: *10 Alscot Road, London SE1 3EJ*

I am writing to advise you that a further complaint has been made against you in respect of:

Unsatisfactory levels of noise

The incident took place on *15 March 2007* at *2am*.

I refer you to our previous correspondence in respect of noise levels and take this opportunity to advise you that continued disruption of the peaceful enjoyment of your neighbours' property by you is unacceptable.

It is therefore my intention to contact the local council to advise them of the repeated complaints that have been made against you regarding this unsociable behaviour.

I have also advised your neighbours to keep a diary of the instances of unsatisfactory levels of noise coming from your property and to report all instances to the council authority.

Please do not hesitate to contact me should you wish to discuss this matter further.

Thank you for your co-operation.

Yours sincerely

Landlord: *A. Landlord*

5.3 NOISE COMPLAINT 3

A. Landlord
76–89 Alscot Road, London SE1 2EA
020 7394 4040

A. Tenant
10 Alscot Road, London SE1 3EJ

Date: *1 May 2007*

Dear *A. Tenant*

Re: *10 Alscot Road, London SE1 3EJ*

I am writing to advise you that a further complaint has been made against you in respect of:

Unsatisfactory levels of noise

The incident took place on *20 April 2007* at *5am*.

I refer you to our previous correspondence in respect of noise levels and take this opportunity to advise you that it is now my intention to report the matter to the district police.

I am also liaising with the local council, which I understand may be monitoring your property for any incidents of unsatisfactory levels of noise.

I take this opportunity to inform you that should any further complaints regarding the above matter be made against you, legal advice will be taken in order to reclaim possession of the property.

I also enclose a Notice Requiring Possession under *Section 21 of the Housing Act 1988*.

Please do not hesitate to contact me should you wish to discuss this matter further.

Thank you for your co-operation in this matter.

Yours sincerely

Landlord: *A. Landlord*

5.4 UNTIDY GARDEN

A. Landlord
76–89 Alscot Road, London SE1 2EA
020 7394 4040

A. Tenant
10 Alscot Road, London SE1 3EJ

Date: *1 May 2007*

Dear *A. Tenant*

Re: *10 Alscot Road, London SE1 3EJ*

I am writing to advise you that the garden areas of the above-named property are not being maintained to a satisfactory standard by you.

Gardens that are not maintained can result in expensive costs if professional services are required to bring them to respectable standards after prolonged periods of misuse.

I therefore respectfully request that you take immediate action to remedy the above and to ensure that the garden is maintained to a reasonable standard.

Should you require contact details for gardeners in your area I would be happy to investigate local tradespersons and provide you with this information.

Please do not hesitate to contact me should you wish to discuss this matter further.

Thank you for your co-operation in this matter.

Yours sincerely

Landlord: *A. Landlord*

5.5 UNAUTHORISED SATELLITE DISH

A. Landlord
76–89 Alscot Road, London SE1 2EA
020 7394 4040

A. Tenant
10 Alscot Road, London SE1 3EJ

Date: *1 May 2007*

Dear *A. Tenant*

Re: *10 Alscot Road, London SE1 3EJ*

I am writing to advise you that you have erected a satellite dish at the above-named property without consent.

*Your property has a restrictive covenant that forbids satellite dishes and other protruding objects from being affixed to the external structure of the building and failure to comply with these regulations can result in expensive charges and costs.**

I therefore respectfully request that you take immediate action to remove the satellite dish and to ensure that a qualified tradesperson is employed to make good to any damage caused.

Please do not hesitate to contact me should you wish to discuss this matter further.

Thank you for your co-operation in this matter.

Yours sincerely

Landlord: *A. Landlord*

[* This paragraph is only to be used if the property is subject to a restrictive covenant.]

5.6 DAMAGE TO EXTERNAL DECORATIONS

A. Landlord
76–89 Alscot Road, London SE1 2EA
020 7394 4040

A. Tenant
10 Alscot Road, London SE1 3EJ

Date: *1 March 2007*

Dear *A. Tenant*

Re: *10 Alscot Road, London SE1 3EJ*

I am writing to advise you that damage has been caused by you to the exterior of the above-named property as described below:

Blocked guttering causing rainwater to overflow down the external wall of the building.

I therefore respectfully request that you take immediate action to ensure that a qualified tradesperson is employed to make good to the damage caused at your cost.

Should you require contact details for tradespersons in your area I would be happy to investigate local contractors and provide you with this information.

I take this opportunity to advise you that failure to repair the above could cause further damage and may result in charges being made to your deposit at the end of the tenancy.

Please do not hesitate to contact me should you wish to discuss this matter further.

Thank you for your co-operation in this matter.

Yours sincerely

Landlord: *A. Landlord*

5.7 DAMAGE TO INTERNAL DECORATIONS

A. Landlord
76–89 Alscot Road, London SE1 2EA
020 7394 4040

A. Tenant
10 Alscot Road, London SE1 3EJ

Date: *1 March 2007*

Dear *A. Tenant*

Re: *10 Alscot Road, London SE1 3EJ*

I am writing to advise you that damage has been caused by you to the interior of the above-named property as described below:

A leak from the door of the washing machine, which is owned by you, is causing damage to the flooring in the kitchen.

I therefore respectfully request that you take immediate action to ensure that a qualified tradesperson is employed to make good to the damage caused at your cost.

Should you require contact details for tradespersons in your area I would be happy to investigate local contractors and provide you with this information.

I take this opportunity to advise you that failure to repair the above could cause further damage and may result in charges being made to your deposit at the end of the tenancy.

Please do not hesitate to contact me should you wish to discuss this matter further.

Thank you for your co-operation in this matter.

Yours sincerely

Landlord: *A. Landlord*

5.8 THREATENING/ANTISOCIAL BEHAVIOUR

A. Landlord
76–89 Alscot Road, London SE1 2EA
020 7394 4040

A. Tenant
10 Alscot Road, London SE1 3EJ

Date: *1 March 2007*

Dear *A. Tenant*

Re: *10 Alscot Road, London SE1 3EJ*

I am writing to advise you that a complaint has been made against you in respect of:

I am informed that you abused and threatened your neighbour for complaining about the noise due to you having a party.

The alleged incident took place on *11 February 2007* at *2am*.

I take this opportunity to advise you that the above constitutes a serious breach of your tenancy and that this matter may be reported to the district police for further investigation.

Should any further complaints regarding the above matter be made against you, legal advice will be taken in order to reclaim possession of the property.

Please do not hesitate to contact me should you wish to discuss this matter further.

Thank you for your co-operation in this matter.

Yours sincerely

Landlord: *A. Landlord*

5.9 SMOKING IN PROPERTY

A. Landlord
76–89 Alscot Road, London SE1 2EA
020 7394 4040

A. Tenant
10 Alscot Road, London SE1 3EJ

Date: *1 March 2007*

Dear *A. Tenant*

Re: *10 Alscot Road, London SE1 3EJ*

I am writing to advise you that you have permitted smoking to take place inside the above-named property and this is unacceptable.

Smoking can cause damage to the internal decorations of the property including yellowing of walls, burning to fabrics and carpets and unpleasant, difficult to remove smells.

I therefore respectfully request that any smoking take place outside the property to ensure that you do not breach the terms of your tenancy agreement.

I take this opportunity to advise you that should work be required to repair damage caused by smoking at the end of your tenancy this may result in charges being made to your deposit.

Please do not hesitate to contact me should you wish to discuss this matter further.

Thank you for your co-operation in this matter.

Yours sincerely

Landlord: *A. Landlord*

5.10 UNAUTHORISED PET IN PROPERTY

A. Landlord
76–89 Alscot Road, London SE1 2EA
020 7394 4040

A. Tenant
10 Alscot Road, London SE1 3EJ

Date: *1 March 2007*

Dear *A. Tenant*

Re: *10 Alscot Road, London SE1 3EJ*

I am writing to advise you that you are keeping a *cat* at the above-named property and this is unacceptable.

Pets can cause damage to the external and internal decorations of the property including fleas and ticks, scratches to fabrics and carpets and in some cases unpleasant, difficult to remove smells.

I therefore respectfully request that any pets be removed from the property immediately to ensure that you do not breach the terms of your tenancy agreement.

No request was made by you to keep a pet at the property and in this instance I can confirm that I would not have granted such permission as the furniture in the property is relatively new and I do not want to risk unnecessary wear or damage.

Please do not hesitate to contact me should you wish to discuss this matter further.

Thank you for your co-operation in this matter.

Yours sincerely

Landlord: *A. Landlord*

5.11 TENANT'S VEHICLE CAUSING DAMAGE TO EXTERNAL GROUNDS

A. Landlord
76–89 Alscot Road, London SE1 2EA
020 7394 4040

A. Tenant
10 Alscot Road, London SE1 3EJ

Date: *1 March 2007*

Dear *A. Tenant*

Re: *10 Alscot Road, London SE1 3EJ*

I am writing to advise you that a vehicle parked at the above-named property is causing damage to the external grounds of the premises as follows:

Oil leaks from your leaking vehicle onto the driveway.

I therefore respectfully request that the vehicle be removed from the property immediately by you and that you instruct a qualified tradesperson to carry out the necessary repairs.

Should you require contact details for tradespersons in your area I would be happy to investigate local contractors and provide you with this information.

I take this opportunity to advise you that should this work not be completed within 14 days a contractor will be instructed privately and the invoice forwarded to you for settlement.

Please do not hesitate to contact me should you wish to discuss this matter further.

Thank you for your co-operation in this matter.

Yours sincerely

Landlord: *A. Landlord*

5.12 TENANT'S VEHICLE PARKED IN UNAUTHORISED AREA

A. Landlord
76–89 Alscot Road, London SE1 2EA
020 7394 4040

A. Tenant
10 Alscot Road, London SE1 3EJ

Date: *1 March 2007*

Dear *A. Tenant*

Re: *10 Alscot Road, London SE1 3EJ*

I am writing to advise you that your vehicle at the above-named property is parked in an unauthorised area as follows:

Your red Mini Cooper, registration number P123 3XA, should not be parked in the spaces reserved for your neighbour, Mr. J. Smith.

I therefore respectfully request that the vehicle be removed from the area immediately and if it is not removed within 14 days, I advise you that the residents' association may take the necessary arrangements to have the vehicle removed without further notice.

If this does occur, you may be required to pay additional impounding and release fees.

Please do not hesitate to contact me should you wish to discuss this matter further.

Thank you for your co-operation in this matter.

Yours sincerely

Landlord: *A. Landlord*

5.13 UNAUTHORISED OCCUPANTS AT PROPERTY

A. Landlord
76–89 Alscot Road, London SE1 2EA
020 7394 4040

A. Tenant
10 Alscot Road, London SE1 3EJ

Date: *1 March 2007*

Dear *A. Tenant*

Re: *10 Alscot Road, London SE1 3EJ*

I am writing to you because it has come to my attention that there are other occupiers currently living with you at the property. Although it is acceptable for visitors to stay with you for short periods, only the tenants named in the tenancy agreement should be living in the property as their home.

If you wish to replace or add a tenant to your agreement, this can only be done if the person or persons concerned have undergone my referencing procedure and been found satisfactory. Please contact me, if appropriate, so that this procedure can be carried out. *However, please note that I am not prepared to allow any change to the named tenants on your tenancy agreement at this time.**

Otherwise* can you please arrange for the unauthorised occupiers to leave within the next 14 days. Your failure to do this may prejudice your tenancy of the property.

Please contact me within the next 14 days to discuss this matter.

Thank you for your co-operation.

Yours sincerely

Landlord: *A. Landlord*

[* Delete if appropriate.]

5.14 FAILURE TO NOTIFY OF REPAIR – TENANT LIABLE

A. Landlord
76–89 Alscot Road, London SE1 2EA
020 7394 4040

A. Tenant
10 Alscot Road, London SE1 3EJ

Date: *1 March 2007*

Dear *A. Tenant*

Re: *10 Alscot Road, London SE1 3EJ*

As you are aware, an appointment was recently made for a contractor known as *A. Contractor* to visit the above-named property to carry out the following work:

Painting the lounge ceiling.

The contractor has carried out the repair and submitted a report stating the cause of the damage was a result of:

The bath leaking for a period of months and destroying the floor and lounge ceiling underneath.

I take this opportunity to advise you that you are liable, as per the terms of your tenancy, to inform me immediately when a repair becomes apparent. In this instance the contractor has confirmed that the damage caused was due to an ongoing need for a repair which could have been carried out earlier.

I therefore enclose a copy of the contractor's invoice (which has been paid), along with a copy of the report and kindly request that you forward a cheque made payable to *A. Landlord* in order that I may close this matter.

I look forward to your remittance by return.

Yours sincerely

Landlord: *A. Landlord*

5.15 REPAIR CARRIED OUT – TENANT LIABLE

A. Landlord
76–89 Alscot Road, London SE1 2EA
020 7394 4040

A. Tenant
10 Alscot Road, London SE1 3EJ

Date: *1 March 2007*

Dear *A. Tenant*

Re: *10 Alscot Road, London SE1 3EJ*

As you are aware, an appointment was recently made for a contractor known as *A. Contractor* to visit the above-named property to carry out the following work:

Replacing bathroom vinyl flooring.

The contractor has carried out the repair and submitted a report stating the cause of the damage was a result of:

The shower screen had been leaking for a long period of time causing damage to the floor.

I take this opportunity to advise you that you are liable, as per the terms of your tenancy, for any damage caused by neglect or misuse of the property.

I therefore enclose a copy of the contractor's invoice (which has been paid), along with a copy of the report and kindly request that you forward a cheque made payable to *A. Landlord* in order that I may close this matter.

I look forward to your remittance by return.

Yours sincerely

Landlord: *A. Landlord*

5.16 TENANT HAS CHANGED LOCKS

A. Landlord
76–89 Alscot Road, London SE1 2EA
020 7394 4040

A. Tenant
10 Alscot Road, London SE1 3EJ

Date: *1 March 2007*

Dear *A. Tenant*

Re: *10 Alscot Road, London SE1 3EJ*

I am writing to advise you that further to a recent visit to the above-named property, it appears that the locks have been changed.

It is important to the security of the property that I ensure that the home is secure and I therefore request that you contact me immediately to confirm if the locks have been changed and the reason the work has taken place.

I will also need to obtain a spare set of keys to the property from you as soon as possible.

Thank you for your co-operation in this matter.

Yours sincerely

Landlord: *A. Landlord*

CHAPTER 6

Handling notices

The nature of the lettings business is that tenants will come and go with some frequency. Sometimes landlords are lucky enough to have tenants that stay in their properties for a number of years, but, at some point during the term of the tenancy, your tenant will decide to vacate the property and will serve you notice to terminate the tenancy.

This chapter deals with how you should approach the receipt of notices to terminate from your tenant and what to do if the notice is unacceptable for any reason. Also, you will find out how mutually to agree to surrender a tenancy and what to do if you think your tenant has abandoned the property.

Notice to terminate a tenancy

In order to give you notice successfully to vacate a property, your tenant must fulfil certain obligations in order to satisfy the terms of the agreement. Some of these terms will be different for each type of tenancy and you should check your agreement to find out the terms that are relevant in your case.

First steps

When you receive a notice offering to terminate the property from your tenant you should check a few things before responding:

- Has the tenant told you the exact date he wishes to vacate?

- Has the tenant given you the proper notice period?

- Is the tenant still held under a fixed-term contract that doesn't allow termination of the tenancy for some time?

- Have all tenants given you notice **and** signed the notice letter?

By answering the above questions you will be able to establish a response to your tenant which will inform him of the next steps involved.

> **Note**
>
> If your tenant is held on an Assured Shorthold Tenancy Agreement, he may have rights to vacate the property on the last day of the fixed term without offering you any notice. Make sure that you keep in touch with your tenant towards the final couple of months of his agreement so that you know whether he intends to leave or not, thus giving you the chance to plan ahead.

A satisfactory offer to terminate the tenancy

If you receive a notice to terminate the property from your tenant which fulfils all of the necessary criteria, you should write to your tenant to confirm what date the final day of the tenancy will be and to advise that you are likely to require access to the property to carry out viewings.

 NOTICE RECEIVED CONFIRMING TENANT'S MOVE-OUT DATE (6.1)

From this point you will need to arrange a check-out with the tenant on the final day that will allow you to go through the Inventory and Schedule of Condition to determine the return of the tenant's deposit.

In order to help the tenant to fulfil the criteria required when moving out of your property and to ensure that there are no claims against his deposit, it's useful to give the tenant clear guidelines, stating what is expected of him on the day of the check-out.

 GUIDANCE NOTES FOR TENANTS VACATING A PROPERTY (6.2)

Note

You cannot ask the tenant to leave the property in a better condition than when he moved in and your tenant is not liable for fair wear and tear that may have occurred during the tenancy. When asking your tenant to carry out tasks detailed in the Guidance Notes you should always consider the standard of the property at the time the tenant took occupancy and be aware that the tenant is not obliged to improve the property.

By sending this information to the tenant you are ensuring that there isn't any confusion over the tenant's duties and you are much more likely to get the property back in a condition which is ready for reletting.

An unsatisfactory offer to terminate the tenancy

In some instances you may find that the notice offering to terminate the property that you have received from your tenant doesn't fulfil all of the obligations as stated in the tenancy agreement.

You should identify where the tenant has failed to meet the relevant criteria and respond accordingly.

Insufficient notice period

If your tenant hasn't given the proper notice period, write to him informing him of this and telling him that he can vacate on the date specified but that he will be responsible for rent up to the end of the notice period he should have given. Tell him that unless he lets you know to the contrary you will assume that he still wishes to vacate on the date specified and will be responsible for the rent to the end of the proper notice period.

 INSUFFICIENT NOTICE PERIOD GIVEN (6.3)

Tenancy still in fixed term

Some tenancy agreements contain clauses that allow landlords and tenants to give notice to each other during the period of the fixed term. Usually referred to as 'break clauses', they are often found in agreements that have had a tenant in occupation for some time and are designed to give flexibility to both parties.

If the agreement doesn't contain a break clause and your tenant wishes to surrender the tenancy during the fixed term of the agreement, normally you won't wish to agree to it. However, under the law there should be some mechanism to allow the tenant to be released from his obligations before the end of the tenancy agreement so long as your rights are not affected, and unless you provide one the tenant may be entitled to assign the tenancy to another tenant. You will not want this, so it's best to permit the tenant to end the tenancy early if he can find a suitable alternative tenant.

You should therefore write to the tenant telling him that you don't consent to him ending the agreement early, unless he is able to find a suitable replacement tenant, who must pass your referencing procedure.

NOTICE RECEIVED BUT DATE UNACCEPTABLE DUE TO FIXED TERM (6.4)

Joint tenancies

Where you have two or more tenants signed up to the same tenancy agreement, all occupants must be considered as a single unit, i.e. 'joint and severally liable'. This means that if either party wishes to vacate the property, they must **all** offer notice to terminate concurrently.

You may, however, decide to be flexible with the tenants if:

* they find a new tenant to replace the outgoing one and sign a new fixed-term contract; or

* the remaining tenant is willing to take the tenancy on in his name only.

If you receive a notice from one of the tenants in the property that informs you of his wish to terminate occupancy, you must respond to **all** of the tenants informing them of the above conditions under which the notice can be accepted.

INDIVIDUAL NOTICE ON A JOINT TENANCY (6.5)

Although it's unlikely, you may be unable to accept notice under the above conditions and you may require all the tenants to give you notice to terminate the property and vacate at the same time. You must inform them in writing of your position so they will be able to make the necessary arrangements. You need to make it clear that they are all liable for the whole of the rent until you have received the property back with vacant possession.

 ALL TENANTS MUST GIVE NOTICE AND VACATE (6.6)

Change of tenants

If you're willing to allow your tenants the option of replacing outgoing tenants or taking the tenancy on in the remaining tenants' names only, it's advisable that you re-reference the tenants. If you do allow a changeover, it's best to set out the terms clearly for this to take place and supply your tenants with the necessary tools to complete the changeover.

Replacement tenants

Find out the name of the person your tenants want to move into the property and send a letter to all existing tenants advising them that you are aware that they wish to make a change to the names on the tenancy agreement.

 CHANGE OF TENANT/S WITH REPLACEMENT/S (6.7)

Remember to include with this letter enough Tenancy Application Forms for **all** tenants to complete and sign as you will need to reference every tenant again before a new tenancy agreement can be signed.

You should also send with the above information a form which details what the tenants must do to satisfy the terms of this transaction. This form also states what will happen with the outgoing tenant's deposit money, and must be signed and dated by all new and existing tenants and returned to you immediately.

 CHANGE OF TENANT/S FORM WITH REPLACEMENT/S (6.8)

No replacement tenants

Sometimes a tenant will wish to leave the property and those who want to remain will request permission to take the tenancy on in their names without the need for finding any replacements.

This is often a simpler transaction, as all you need to do is have all parties to be in agreement with the proposed changeover and re-reference the remaining tenants.

Write to all your existing tenants confirming the planned changes to those named on the agreement and enclose the necessary Tenancy Application Forms.

You need to make it clear that the outgoing tenant will remain liable for the rent until a new tenancy agreement has been signed by the remaining tenants.

 CHANGE OF TENANT/S WITHOUT REPLACEMENT/S (6.9)

Also enclose with the above the necessary form which details what will happen to the outgoing tenant's deposit and the terms for the transaction to take place successfully. This must be signed by all of the tenants and returned immediately.

 CHANGE OF TENANT/S FORM WITHOUT REPLACEMENT/S (6.10)

Note

Always re-reference your tenants (and guarantors) before the start of a new tenancy agreement. If the financial situation of the tenant changes during the course of his existing tenancy, this might affect your decision to offer him a new contract. Remember that tenants can lose their jobs or run up debts whilst they are living at your property and if you offer a new tenancy agreement to somebody who is unable to pay the rent, you risk serious financial loss.

Breaking the tenancy

There are times where it's convenient for both parties to agree to terminate the tenancy agreement outside of the terms set out in the contract and it's possible for a landlord and tenant mutually to agree for this to take place by arrangement.

The most common reason for mutually terminating a tenancy agreement is where the landlord is selling the property and the tenant has found somewhere else to go. Alternatively, it might be your tenant who is buying a property and you have a new applicant willing to replace him quickly.

It's important that you and your tenant sign a document to state your intentions to agree to terminate the current tenancy and to release each other from any further obligations stated in the contract.

MUTUAL RELEASE OF TENANCY (6.11)

Tip

Don't commit to mutually terminating the tenancy until you have secured everything you need to facilitate a beneficial changeover. If you have to replace an outgoing tenant, make sure that all the paperwork is signed and that the replacement tenant is ready to move in.

Note

Always have a witness who can confirm what you have agreed. A witness should be present at all discussions and formal meetings regarding this matter and should be asked to sign and date all documents pertaining to the mutual release of a tenancy.

Tip

Notwithstanding any agreement reached with the tenant, you shouldn't sign any binding documentation regarding the sale of the property until you have vacant possession because if the tenant breaks his agreement and fails to vacate, this would put you in breach of contract with the purchaser and potentially liable for damages for breach of contract. It may not be possible practically to recover this from the tenant.

Abandonment

Although it's quite uncommon, tenants will sometimes vacate your property without giving you any notice or returning the keys to you or telling you where they have gone. This is known as 'abandonment'.

Unfortunately, a tenant who has abandoned your property is likely to have other ongoing issues with you and the terms of his tenancy. In many circumstances a tenant will have rent arrears, may be facing court proceedings against him in respect of financial claims or could have caused damage to your property which he cannot repair.

If you have been trying to contact your tenant in writing, by telephone and/or by email for whatever reason and you have received no reply, this is an indication that the tenant is either ignoring you or is no longer contactable with the details that you have on file. You should arrange to go to the property to carry out a routine visit to see if the tenant is still in occupation.

Note

Don't assume that you can visit the property without giving the proper notice in writing to your tenant. Although you may be anxious to check on the status of the tenant, you must not breach the terms of the tenancy agreement and your tenant's rights regarding access.

When you visit the property there are number of things to look out for that could indicate your tenant has abandoned and may give you a clue as to the last time he was in the property:

- Unopened mail piling up behind the door or in the letterbox
- Keys left behind
- Demands for payment of outstanding invoices
- Out-of-date food in the fridge
- No clothing in the wardrobes
- Old newspapers

Tip

Always take somebody with you who can independently witness the condition of the property and your findings. Complete a Property Visit Report and ask the witness to read and sign it at the property.

If at this stage you suspect your tenant to have abandoned the property, it is advisable that you should make an application to the court for possession or instruct a solicitor to act on your behalf.

Alternatively...

If it's absolutely clear that the tenant has vacated the property, i.e. he has removed all personal items and left behind his keys, you may consider posting a Notice of Abandonment to the main access points of the property, which confirms your status as owner of the property and declares your intent to reclaim possession within the stated timeframe (usually 14 days from the date of the notice) unless the tenant contacts you to advise otherwise. If you have a justified fear that the property isn't secure, you can fit a new lock, but you must state in the notice where the tenant will be able to get the keys and under no circumstances should you refuse your tenant re-entry.

 NOTICE OF ABANDONMENT (6.12)

Beware!

It's possible that your tenant may have taken an extended holiday or he could be in hospital or in prison and be unable to make contact with you. In any of these instances it's unreasonable for you to retake possession. You should only consider using a Notice of Abandonment when you are absolutely sure that the tenant has left the property and is not going to return. The Notice of Abandonment isn't a legal document and is not supported by any legal framework. If you take possession of a property which hasn't been abandoned, your tenant may be able to make a civil claim against you to take back possession of the property. The tenant may also include a claim for financial damages in respect of breach of contract and in some cases you could face criminal prosecution from the local authority for an offence under the Protection from Eviction Act 1977.

If you're considering posting a Notice of Abandonment, you should assess the risks in each case. Making a claim for possession through the courts may take longer, but if the property is repossessed by bailiffs after you have obtained an order for possession, then you are well protected against any claims. If in doubt, seek advice from a solicitor qualified in landlord and tenant law.

Don't forget...

Notices displayed in easy view of the public which state that your property is empty could be an advertisement for squatters! This is obviously less likely for an apartment within a secure building or a room in a shared house, but you should strongly consider this risk if you decide to post a Notice of Abandonment.

6.1 NOTICE RECEIVED CONFIRMING TENANT'S MOVE-OUT DATE

A. Landlord
76–89 Alscot Road, London SE1 2EA
020 7394 4040

A. Tenant
10 Alscot Road, London SE1 3EJ

Date: *1 March 2007*

Dear *A. Tenant*

Re: *10 Alscot Road, London SE1 3EJ*

I am writing to confirm that your offer of Notice in respect of the above-named property has been received and your final date of occupancy will be as follows:

31 May 2007

I have enclosed a set of 'Guidance Notes for Tenants Vacating a Property' to assist you in completing the required procedure and kindly request that you contact me at your earliest convenience to arrange a time to complete a check-out with you on the day.

I may require access to your property in order to carry out viewings with prospective new tenants and I will contact you in advance with any appointments.

I look forward to hearing from you.

Yours sincerely

Landlord: *A. Landlord*

6.2 GUIDANCE NOTES FOR TENANTS VACATING A PROPERTY

These notes have been designed to assist you when handing your property back to the landlord at the check-out appointment.

In order to protect your deposit against claims being made, it's advisable that you read these guidelines and take the appropriate action.

If you have any questions regarding the check-out or you require a duplicate copy of your inventory, please contact your landlord immediately.

- Ensure that the property has been left in a good, clean condition throughout and all of your personal items have been completely removed.

- All items should be returned to exactly the same position as they are listed on your Inventory.

- All windows, mirrors and glass items should be cleaned and polished.

- All woodwork, skirting, dado rails, picture rails, frames, shelving and cabinets, etc. should be cleaned and polished.

- All soft furnishings, such as carpets, curtains, rugs, bed linen, towels, throws and mattresses, etc. should be laundered/washed free of stains, ironed (where applicable) and left clean.

- All walls and ceilings should be dusted, wiped over (where necessary) and free of excessive wear.

- All kitchen appliances, including cookers, hobs, microwave ovens, toasters, washing machines, tumble dryers, etc. should be cleaned free of residues, grease and stains.

- All kitchen cupboards should be cleaned and emptied of your food and belongings.

- Fridges and freezers should be emptied of food, cleaned thoroughly, defrosted, switched off and doors left open.

- Bathrooms should be cleaned thoroughly and all sealant and grouting should be free of staining or mould.

- All light bulbs should be present and in working order.

- All picture hooks, tacks, screws, nails or other fittings installed by you should be removed and any damage made good.

- Gardens should be in a well-maintained condition for the time of year, lawns should be cut and all garden implements should be clean and in working order.

6.2 GUIDANCE NOTES FOR TENANTS VACATING A PROPERTY (continued)

- Any missing or damaged items should be replaced to match.

- Utility companies and local authorities should be contacted by you with meter readings on the final day of your tenancy.

- All mail received addressed to you after you have vacated the property will be returned to sender.

Thank you for your co-operation.

6.3 NOTICE RECEIVED BUT INSUFFICIENT NOTICE PERIOD GIVEN

A. Landlord
76–89 Alscot Road, London SE1 2EA
020 7394 4040

A. Tenant
10 Alscot Road, London SE1 3EJ

Date: *31 May 2007*

Dear *A. Tenant*

Re: *10 Alscot Road, London SE1 3EJ*

I am writing to confirm that your offer of Notice in respect of the above-named property has been received. However, the date that you have offered to terminate your tenancy cannot be accepted for the following reason:

You are required to give *one month's notice* to terminate your tenancy.

I therefore take this opportunity to advise you that the final day of your tenancy will be:

30 June 2007.

I have enclosed a set of 'Guidance Notes for Tenants Vacating a Property' to assist you in completing the required procedure and kindly request that you contact me at your earliest convenience to arrange a time to complete a check-out with you on the day.

I may require access to your property in order to carry out viewings with prospective new tenants and I will contact you in advance with any appointments.

I look forward to hearing from you.

Yours sincerely

Landlord: *A. Landlord*

6.4 NOTICE RECEIVED BUT DATE UNACCEPTABLE DUE TO FIXED TERM

A. Landlord
76–89 Alscot Road, London SE1 2EA
020 7394 4040

A. Tenant
10 Alscot Road, London SE1 3EJ

Date: *1 May 2007*

Dear *A. Tenant*

Re: *10 Alscot Road, London SE1 3EJ*

I am writing to confirm that your offer of Notice in respect of the above-named property has been received. However, the date that you have offered to terminate your tenancy cannot be accepted for the following reason:

You are currently held on a fixed-term tenancy agreement that doesn't expire until *31 July 2007* and your tenancy agreement does not contain a break clause.

If you wish to vacate before the end of the term, you will be responsible for the rent until a new tenant can be found, plus my reasonable costs. Alternatively, if you can suggest a new tenant to take your place, I will agree to the early termination of your tenancy, subject to the replacement tenant satisfying my referencing requirements and agreeing to take on a tenancy of the property for a period not less than the remainder of your fixed term.

Please let me know whether you still wish to vacate on the date given in your Notice. If you wish to propose a replacement tenant, please ask him to contact me at the above address.

Thank you for your co-operation.

Yours sincerely

Landlord: *A. Landlord*

6.5 INDIVIDUAL NOTICE ON A JOINT TENANCY

A. Landlord
76–89 Alscot Road, London SE1 2EA
020 7394 4040

A. Tenant
10 Alscot Road, London SE1 3EJ

Date: *1 March 2007*

Dear *A. Tenant*

Re: *10 Alscot Road, London SE1 3EJ*

I am writing to confirm that your offer of Notice in respect of the above-named property has been received.

As you are currently signed to a tenancy agreement that holds all tenants joint and severally liable, in this case your Notice can only be accepted on the following terms:

- Those tenants that wish to remain at the property must offer to take the tenancy on in full and agree to release those who want to leave. This is subject to conditions, however, and may involve re-referencing of remaining tenants to ensure that financial abilities to maintain the level of rent can be achieved.

Or

- You may wish to find new tenants to replace those who would like to leave and I ask that if this is the case you present new prospective tenants so that referencing procedures can take place. New tenants will only be accepted if they fulfil the required referencing criteria.

I take this opportunity to advise you that no tenants can be released from the tenancy agreement until the above has taken place and a new tenancy agreement has been signed by all parties. Note that until a new tenancy agreement has been signed, all existing tenants will remain liable for the rent **whether or not they are actually living at the property**.

Please do not hesitate to contact me should you wish to discuss this matter further.

Yours sincerely

Landlord: *A. Landlord*

6.6 ALL TENANTS MUST GIVE NOTICE AND VACATE

A. Landlord
76–89 Alscot Road, London SE1 2EA
020 7394 4040

A. Tenant
10 Alscot Road, London SE1 3EJ

Date: *1 March 2007*

Dear *A. Tenant*

Re: *10 Alscot Road, London SE1 3EJ*

I am writing to confirm that your offer of Notice in respect of the above-named property has been received. However, I am unable to accept the offer to terminate the tenancy for the following reason:

You are currently signed to a tenancy agreement that holds all tenants joint and severally liable, which means that you must all give notice together to terminate the property.

As you are a joint tenant, unless all the tenants vacate the property at the same time, you will all remain liable for the rent under the tenancy agreement that you signed, whether or not you are actually living at the property.

Please do not hesitate to contact me should you wish to discuss this matter further.

Yours sincerely

Landlord: *A. Landlord*

6.7 CHANGE OF TENANT/S WITH REPLACEMENT/S

A. Landlord
76–89 Alscot Road, London SE1 2EA
020 7394 4040

A. Tenant
10 Alscot Road, London SE1 3EJ

Date: *1 March 2007*

Dear *A. Tenant*

Re: *10 Alscot Road, London SE1 3EJ*

Further to your recent correspondence, I understand that you wish to make changes to those named on your tenancy agreement.

My records show that *A. Tenant* wishes to vacate the property and that you have a replacement tenant known as *A. Tenant 2* who would like to make an application.

Please therefore find enclosed Tenancy Application Forms for all remaining and all new tenants in respect of the above.

Also enclosed is a Change of Tenant/s with Replacement/s Form which needs to be completed by all new and existing tenants.

I kindly request that you return the enclosed documents as soon as possible in order that the application can be processed.

Please do not hesitate to contact me should you wish to discuss this matter further.

Yours sincerely

Landlord: *A. Landlord*

6.8 CHANGE OF TENANT/S FORM WITH REPLACEMENT/S

Property address: _____

_____

_____

Current tenant/s:_____

_____

It is hereby agreed that we, the above named, accept that the following tenant/s: _____

_____

Wish/es to vacate the property on: _____

And for new tenant/s named: _____

_____

To make a tenancy application.

We understand that all remaining and new tenants are required to complete an application procedure for the new tenancy and we agree that the outgoing tenant/s cannot be released from the existing contract until such time as all references have been received with satisfactory information, all rent is paid up to date, a new tenancy agreement has been signed by all tenants and this form has been signed and returned to the landlord.

A check-out cannot take place in between the tenancies and we therefore agree to acquit the outgoing tenant/s from any claims whatsoever that may arise in this and any other matters. The deposit will continue to be held in full and, if necessary, we agree to settle any balances with the outgoing tenant/s for monies that they may have paid at the commencement of the existing tenancy.

Signed by all existing tenants: _____

_____

_____

Signed by all tenants: _____

_____

_____

Date: _____

6.9 CHANGE OF TENANT/S WITHOUT REPLACEMENT/S

A. Landlord
76–89 Alscot Road, London SE1 2EA
020 7394 4040

A. Tenant
10 Alscot Road, London SE1 3EJ

Date: *1 March 2007*

Dear *A. Tenant*

Re: *10 Alscot Road, London SE1 3EJ*

Further to your recent correspondence, I understand that you wish to make changes to those named on your tenancy agreement.

Our records show that *A. Tenant 2* wishes to vacate the property and that *A. Tenant 1 and A. Tenant 3* would like to take on the tenancy in their name only.

Please therefore find enclosed a 'Tenancy Application Form' for the remaining tenants in respect of the above.

Also enclosed is a 'Change of Tenant Without Replacement Form', which needs to be completed by all of the tenants.

I kindly request that you return the enclosed documents as soon as possible in order that the application can be processed.

Please do not hesitate to contact me should you wish to discuss this matter further.

Yours sincerely

Landlord: *A. Landlord*

6.10 CHANGE OF TENANT/S FORM WITHOUT REPLACEMENT/S

Property address: _____

_____

_____

Current tenant/s: _____

_____

It is hereby agreed that we, the above named, accept that the following tenant/s: _____

_____

Wish/es to vacate the property on: _____

And that the remaining tenant/s wishes to take the property on without replacements.

We understand that all remaining tenants are required to complete an application procedure for the new tenancy and we agree that the outgoing tenant/s cannot be released from the existing contract until such time as all references have been received with satisfactory information, all rent is paid up to date, a new tenancy agreement has been signed by all tenants and this form has been signed and returned to the landlord.

A check-out cannot take place in between the tenancies and we therefore agree to acquit the outgoing tenant/s from any claims whatsoever that may arise in this and any other matters. The deposit will continue to be held in full and, if necessary, we agree to settle any balances with the outgoing tenant/s for monies that they have paid at the commencement of the existing tenancy.

Signed by all existing tenants: _____

_____

_____

Date: _____

6.11 MUTUAL RELEASE OF TENANCY

Property address: _____

_____

_____

It is hereby agreed between:

_____(the landlord)

And:

_____(the tenant)

That the tenancy agreement in respect of the above-named property which began on:

_____

Shall be terminated on:

_____

And that both parties will acquit each other of any claims whatsoever in respect of the previous tenancy on the following conditions:

• Rent due has been settled by the tenant up to the date of the agreement.
• The property is returned to the landlord without damage and there is no cause for the landlord to make financial claims against the tenant for breach of tenancy. (If a financial claim is to be made by the landlord, the sum shall not be limited by the amount held as deposit.)

Signed by the landlord: _____

Signed by the tenant/s: _____

_____

_____

In the presence of (witness): _____

_____

_____

Name and address of witness: _____

_____

_____

6.12 NOTICE OF INTENTION TO RECLAIM POSSESSION OF AN ABANDONED PROPERTY

Date: _____

Name of tenant/s: _____

_____

_____

Property address: _____

_____

_____

As landlord of this property, I/we believe that the current tenant has vacated without giving notice and I/we therefore intend to take back possession.

I/we have visited the property today and found it to be unoccupied.

The locks have been changed for security reasons and if the tenant should return within the notice period given below, keys will be available at our address.

If anyone has information relating to the tenant's whereabouts, please contact me/us before the expiry of this notice.

If the tenant does not return within the notice period given below, I/we will, as landlord/s of this property, take back possession and assume that the tenant has given up the property.

If the tenant does return within the notice period given below, he will have rights to regain entry to the property and take possession.

Name: _____

Address: _____

_____

Tel: _____

Name of witness: _____

Signature of witness: _____

Date I/we plan to reclaim possession: _____

CHAPTER 7

Check-out and deposit return

In the final stages of the tenancy you will be expected to perform a check-out of the property with the Inventory and Schedule of Condition and you will account to the tenant for the sum of the deposit that was given at the commencement of the agreement.

It's at this point that many landlords find themselves in disagreement with the tenant and are struggling to resolve a dispute over what should happen with the deposit money. However, on 6 April 2007 the Government launched a new scheme that applies to all Assured Shorthold Tenancies in England and Wales where a deposit is taken.

Assured Shorthold Tenancies that commenced before the launch date are not required to take part but you must still ensure that you act professionally and reasonably when undertaking the task of checking your tenant out of the property and administering the return of the deposit.

Tenancy deposit protection

Tenancy deposit protection (TDP) is designed to ensure that the methods of handling a tenant's deposit are improved whilst assisting in the resolution of deposit-related disputes and promoting good practice, such as clear inventories provided to tenants.

All landlords must comply with the regulations and are required to join either a single custodial scheme or one of two insurance-based schemes that have been authorised by the Government:

1. The Deposit Protection Service (DPS) – a custodial scheme

Within 14 days of receiving the tenant's deposit you must, as landlord, pay the deposit into the free-to-use scheme and inform your tenant in the prescribed form which scheme you are using. Confirmation of receipt will also be sent by the DPS to both you and your tenant. At the end of the tenancy, if you and your tenant are in agreement about the way the deposit should be divided, you will both be required to inform the tenancy deposit scheme who will administer the return accordingly within ten days. If there is a dispute between you and your tenant over the division of the deposit, the tenancy deposit scheme will hold the disputed sum and pass your case to the Dispute Resolution Service or the courts for adjudication and final settlement.

For more information about DPS, visit www.depositprotection.com.

2. Tenancy Deposit Solutions Ltd (TDSL) and the Tenancy Deposit Scheme (TDS) – insurance-based schemes

These schemes allow the landlord to retain the tenant's deposit. However, you must pay a premium to the insurer (either TDSL or TDS) and within 14 days of receiving the deposit from your tenant you must inform him in the prescribed form which scheme you are using. At the end of the tenancy, if you and your tenant agree how the deposit should be divided, you will administer the return accordingly. If either you or your tenant disputes the amount, however, you must hand over the disputed sum to the scheme pending adjudication and final settlement.

For more information about TDSL, visit www.mydeposits.co.uk or for TDS, visit www.tds.gb.com.

Be prepared

In most instances where a dispute is registered with either scheme you will be required to substantiate your claims for the amount you want to deduct from the tenant's deposit. You will be asked to provide information such as:

- the precise reasons for the amount you wish to deduct;
- a signed Inventory and Schedule of Condition;

- Guidance Notes for Tenants Vacating a Property (see page 118) provided to your tenant;

- a schedule of costs, copies of quotes, estimates and invoices, etc.

Failure to provide any of the above could affect your ability to successfully retain sums of the tenant's deposit regardless of whether damage or loss has taken place.

For more information and a step-by-step guide to creating an Inventory and Schedule of Condition, see Lawpack's website at www.lawpack.co.uk.

Penalties

In the event that you fail to use one of the schemes or if you don't notify your tenant of the scheme that you have chosen, the Government has implemented penalties which could seriously affect your ability to manage the tenancy and could cost you a lot of money.

Under tenancy deposit protection if the fixed term of the tenancy has expired and you haven't safeguarded the tenant's deposit accordingly or informed the tenant in the prescribed manner, you will be unable to regain possession of the property by giving the tenant the usual minimum two months' notice in writing in accordance with Section 21 of the Housing Act 1988.

Your tenant may also apply to the courts for an order that forces you to place the deposit in one of the schemes and if he is successful, you will also be ordered to pay the tenant **three times** the sum of the deposit in compensation!

For more information about tenancy deposit protection, visit www. communities.gov.uk or contact 020 7944 4400.

The check-out procedure

You should make sure that whenever possible the check-out of the property is performed no later than 24 hours after the final day of the tenancy in order to ensure that no external forces have had time to impact on the condition of the property which has been left by your tenant.

For example, this could give your tenant a potential defence to any claim you may make (e.g. in the County court), as he could allege that he wasn't responsible for the damage and that it was done after he had left.

The check-out should be performed as follows:

1. Meet the tenant at the property.

2. Go through the Inventory and Schedule of Condition that the tenant signed at the commencement of the tenancy.

3. Make notes on the Inventory document and complete a Check-Out Report that shows where any changes or instances of damage have occurred to the property.

4. Ask your tenant to sign the Check-Out Report to confirm that your comments are a fair and accurate statement.

5. Take the keys and forwarding address from the tenant.

6. Take meter readings (see chapter 8).

7. Send a copy of the Check-Out Report to the tenant.

8. Send letters to utility companies and council bodies advising of a change of occupancy.

9. Account to the tenant with regard to the deposit money.

Note

You must have a documented account of how the property was presented to your tenant at the start of the tenancy, signed by the tenant. Otherwise, it will be difficult to defend deductions (e.g. in the context of a County court claim for the recovery of the deposit by the tenant or through the tenancy deposit protection scheme). If the only evidence is your word against the tenant's, the person responsible for adjudicating on final settlement may choose to believe the tenant.

If you have performed a check-out and you can see no reason to make any claims against the tenant's deposit, you shouldn't waste time in administering the return of the money in full. As long as you have the full sets of keys and a forwarding address there is no need to hold on to the deposit and you can skip step 7 above.

If the tenancy started after 6 April 2007, depending on which scheme you have opted for to safeguard the tenant's deposit, you will either contact the relevant administrators to arrange for the money to be returned (custodial scheme) or you will return the deposit yourself (insurance-based schemes).

In some circumstances it may be difficult for a tenant to provide you with a forwarding address. However, this shouldn't in any way hold up the process of the deposit return and you should liaise with the tenant over the best way to hand back the deposit money.

If you are holding the deposit yourself, write a cheque for the balance and send it on to the tenant's forwarding address within ten days with a covering letter.

 DEPOSIT RETURN IN FULL (7.1)

If the deposit is held by a tenancy deposit protection scheme, write to the tenant informing him that you have authorised the full amount to be returned.

 DEPOSIT RETURN IN FULL – TDP (7.2)

> **Tip**
>
> If you are registered with one of the tenancy deposit protection insurance schemes or the tenancy started prior to 6 April 2007, don't bring cash to the check-out. You don't know what you might find when you get to the property and carrying large sums of cash presents a security risk to both parties. A cheque sent to the tenant's forwarding address is safer and will ensure that the tenant gives you the best contact address for the changing of utility suppliers and council bodies!

The Check-Out Report

This document should clearly detail your findings with respect of any damages or areas where the tenant has failed to maintain the terms of the check-out and confirm if you intend to make a claim against the tenant's deposit.

 CHECK-OUT REPORT (7.3)

You should send this report to your tenant within **seven days** of the check-out with a covering letter and a breakdown of costs that you wish to make against his deposit. If the tenancy started before 6 April 2007, you need to advise your tenant that you intend to make specific deductions from his deposit.

 CHECK-OUT REPORT COVERING LETTER (7.4)

If your tenant's deposit is part of a protection scheme, you will need to advise him of what action you will take next if he disputes the amounts claimed.

 CHECK-OUT REPORT COVERING LETTER – TDP (7.5)

For more information about how to calculate costs, see 'Making deductions' below.

> **Tip**
>
> You should always obtain at least two quotes for work to be carried out and keep these documents for six years after the tenant has vacated.

Making deductions

When you intend to make a deduction against the tenant's deposit you must consider the items that you are claiming for very carefully and you must always take into account the age and value of the items in respect of depreciation and wear.

It's easy to work out how much it costs to clean the property, but if you want to make a claim for damaged or missing items you must consider the following:

- How much money the item costs new

- The expected lifespan of the item that is damaged or missing

- How long the item had been in the property before the tenant took occupancy

- The condition of the item when the tenant took occupancy

Example

A tenant vacates a property after breaking an armchair and spilling red wine all over the seats. The item of furniture has been damaged beyond repair and the landlord wants to claim for a replacement against the tenant's deposit.

The first thing the landlord must do is find out how much the armchair would cost to replace if it were new: **The cost of a similar armchair is £300.**

The landlord must now consider how long an armchair might naturally last in a rented property before replacement is required: **Let's say five years.**

Now the landlord needs to work out how long the armchair had been in the property when the tenant moved in: **The armchair was new three years ago.**

And finally, the condition of the armchair when this particular tenant took occupancy: **Good condition.**

The landlord now has all of the information required to make a reasonable claim against the tenant's deposit by following this simple equation:

Cost New ÷ Natural Life Span × No. Years of Lost Usage = Amount to Claim

In our example this would work out as follows:

300 ÷ 5 × 3 = 180

As the armchair was in good condition when the tenant moved in, it would not be reasonable to argue that there was any wear outside of normal boundaries that could lower the amount claimed by the landlord.

The landlord cannot claim for the usage already had from the item and it's unreasonable to claim 'old for new' even where the item was in good condition at the start of the tenancy.

By taking these elements into account and working in this way you can provide your tenant with a claim which should be reasonable and fair.

Chasing acceptance of the claim

If you have sent a letter to your tenant which details the deductions that you intend to make against his deposit, you can expect to receive a response from him within the timescale you have provided.

If, however, your tenant has failed to contact you, don't assume that your claim has been accepted. Either send a second letter informing him that you will administer his deposit release according to your claim if you don't hear from him, for example, within a further **five working days** (**CHASING TENANT FOR ACCEPTANCE OF PROPOSED DEDUCTIONS (7.6)**) or, in the instance that the deposit is safeguarded, contact the administrator of the tenancy deposit protection scheme and seek advice on how best to proceed. It may be necessary for you to pass the matter on entirely for adjudication and final settlement in which case you can relax and wait for a decision.

Dispute

If your tenant wishes to dispute the deductions that you intend to make against the deposit, you should request a reason for the tenant's disagreement.

If the tenant has provided you with this information, you must make a decision as to how you wish to proceed.

If you are in disagreement with the entire dispute your tenant has raised and you are confident that the deductions you are making are fair and reasonable, then you should pass the matter on to the administrator of the tenancy deposit protection scheme that is safeguarding the tenant's deposit and advise your tenant accordingly. You should also enclose a cheque to the tenant for the undisputed sum of the deposit.

DISPUTE OF CLAIM RECEIVED – DISAGREEMENT AND NOTIFICATION OF ASSIGNMENT TO TDP (7.7)

If, however, the tenancy started before 6 April 2007 and the tenant's deposit is not safeguarded, you may wish to return the deposit minus your deductions with a letter explaining your actions to the tenant.

DISPUTE OF CLAIM RECEIVED – DISAGREEMENT (7.8)

Beware!

Your tenant may decide to sue you for withholding sums of his deposit which he doesn't agree with. You should only return a deposit minus deductions where you have either obtained the tenant's consent to do so or, in the instance that the tenancy commenced prior to 6 April 2007, you are absolutely confident that the deductions you are making are fair. If your tenant takes you to the Small Claims Court, you should be prepared for a judge to be tough on you and be expected to justify each deduction you have made, proving that you are entitled to make the deductions and that the amounts you have taken are reasonable.

If your tenant has made an argument that you feel is partially reasonable and brings to your attention an area that you hadn't considered in your initial claim, you may wish to re-evaluate your claim. If this is the case, you should respond to your tenant with the details of your amended claim and again try to obtain his approval within a further **five working days** so that you can administer the return of the deposit accordingly.

 DISPUTE OF CLAIM RECEIVED – PARTIAL AGREEMENT (7.9)

Acceptance of the claim

Once you have been able to agree the claim to be made against the deposit and you have the tenant's written consent to proceed you should make the necessary arrangements by either sending a cheque to the forwarding address that you have been provided with (**DEPOSIT RETURN MINUS DEDUCTIONS (7.10)**) or contact the administrator of the tenancy deposit protection scheme that is safeguarding the tenant's deposit for settlement.

 DEPOSIT RETURN MINUS DEDUCTIONS – AUTHORISATION SENT TO TDP (7.11)

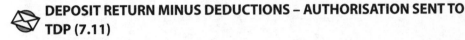

Continued dispute

If you have been unable to reach an agreement with your tenant regarding the claim that you are making against the deposit, you should either seek professional advice or, in the instance that the tenancy began after 6 April 2007, pass the matter on to the administrator of the tenancy deposit scheme that safeguards your tenant's deposit.

Deposit disputes that go to court can be time-consuming and expensive and it's never guaranteed that the result will be in your favour.

Some landlords will consider that they have made a fair and reasonable claim even after the tenant continues to dispute them and will proceed with administering the settlement of the tenant's deposit according to their workings.

If a cheque that you send to the tenant is cashed, it could be assumed that he has accepted your claim but you should beware when making the decision to proceed without the tenant's authority.

If the tenant decides to take you to court and you have failed in your assessment of the claim, you may be told to compensate the tenant for the money you have taken as well as paying the costs incurred by the tenant in pursuing you.

7.1 DEPOSIT RETURN IN FULL

A. Landlord
76–89 Alscot Road, London SE1 2EA
020 7394 4040

A. Tenant
10 Alscot Road, London SE1 3EJ

Date: *1 March 2007*

Dear *A. Tenant*

Re: *10 Alscot Road, London SE1 3EJ*

Please find enclosed a cheque for the sum of *£800* being the return of your deposit in full in respect of the above-named property.

I trust that this is satisfactory and I take this opportunity to wish you all the best for your future.

Yours sincerely

Landlord: *A. Landlord*

7.2 DEPOSIT RETURN IN FULL – TDP

A. Landlord
76–89 Alscot Road, London SE1 2EA
020 7394 4040

A. Tenant
10 Alscot Road, London SE1 3EJ

Date: *1 March 2007*

Dear *A. Tenant*

Re: *10 Alscot Road, London SE1 3EJ*

Further to the recent check-out that was carried out in respect of the above-named property, I am pleased to advise you that I have forwarded written authorisation to the tenancy deposit protection service that safeguards your deposit to return the full amount to you.

I understand that a cheque will be forwarded to you within approximately ten days of receipt of the information.

I trust that this is satisfactory and I take this opportunity to wish you all the best for your future.

Yours sincerely

Landlord: *A. Landlord*

7.3 CHECK-OUT REPORT

Property address: _____

_____

_____

Date of check-out: _____

Name/s of tenant/s: _____

_____

Dates of tenancy:

Start: _____ End: _____

Tenant/s present at check-out: ☐ Yes ☐ No

New contact/forwarding address of tenant/s: _____

_____

_____

_____

_____

_____

Amount of deposit held: £ _____

Utility meter readings at check-out:

Gas: _____

Electric: _____

Water: _____

Condition of property at check-out: _____

_____

_____

_____

_____

_____

_____

_____

_____

7.3 CHECK-OUT REPORT (continued)

Any action required and timescales to account to tenant: _____

_____

_____

_____

_____

_____

_____

_____

_____

_____

_____

Will a financial claim be made against the deposit? ☐ Yes ☐ No

Name:_____(Landlord)

Date: _____

Signed:_____

7.4 CHECK-OUT REPORT COVERING LETTER

A. Landlord
76–89 Alscot Road, London SE1 2EA
020 7394 4040

A. Tenant
10 Alscot Road, London SE1 3EJ

Date: *1 May 2007*

Dear *A. Tenant*

Re: *10 Alscot Road, London SE1 3EJ*

Further to the recent check-out that was carried out at the above-named property, I enclose a copy of the report for your attention.

I take this opportunity to advise you that it is my intention to make a claim against your deposit in accordance with this report and I hereby provide a breakdown of the claim as follows:

Description	Total Cost in £	Amount Claimed in £
Cleaning	100.00	100.00
Replace armchair	300.00	180.00 (3/5)
Burn on carpet	n/a	20.00 (compensation)
TOTAL	400.00	300.00

[Insert details of why you are making the claim:]

* *The property required thorough cleaning and the cost of this work amounted to £100, for which a copy of the invoice is enclosed for your information.*

* *The armchair was damaged beyond repair and the claim considers that the full life of the item would be approximately five years. The rug was two years old when you moved into the property and was presented in good condition at that time. The claim therefore reflects the cost of replacement minus the use already benefited from it. Please see documentation confirming the full cost of the item.*

* *The cigarette burn in the carpet is claimed as a compensatory figure of £20 and this sum is, I believe, less than the cost of an apportioned claim for replacement of the entire carpet.*

7.4 CHECK-OUT REPORT COVERING LETTER (continued)

In the interest of fairness, I kindly request that you consider the above claim to be reasonable and that you confirm instructions to proceed with the disbursement of the deposit accordingly.

I trust that this is satisfactory.

Yours sincerely

Landlord: *A. Landlord*

7.5 CHECK-OUT REPORT COVERING LETTER – TDP

A. Landlord
76–89 Alscot Road, London SE1 2EA
020 7394 4040

A. Tenant
10 Alscot Road, London SE1 3EJ

Date: *1 March 2007*

Dear *A. Tenant*

Re: *10 Alscot Road, London SE1 3EJ*

Further to the recent check-out that was carried out at the above-named property, I enclose a copy of the report for your attention.

I take this opportunity to advise you that it is my intention to make a claim against your deposit in accordance with this report and I hereby provide a breakdown of the claim as follows:

Description	Total Cost in £	Amount Claimed in £
Cleaning	100.00	100.00
Replace armchair	300.00	180.00 (3/5)
Burn on carpet	n/a	20.00 (compensation)
TOTAL	400.00	300.00

[Insert details of why you are making the claim:]

- *The property required thorough cleaning and the cost of this work amounted to £100 for which a copy of the invoice is enclosed for your information.*

- *The armchair was damaged beyond repair and the claim considers that the full life of the item would be approximately five years. The rug was two years old when you moved into the property and was presented in good condition at that time. The claim therefore reflects the cost of replacement minus the use already benefited from it. Please see documentation confirming the full cost of the item.*

- *The cigarette burn in the carpet is claimed as a compensatory figure of £20 and this sum is, I believe, less than the cost of an apportioned claim for replacement of the entire carpet.*

7.5 CHECK-OUT REPORT COVERING LETTER – TDP (continued)

In the interest of fairness, I kindly request that you consider the above claim to be reasonable and that you confirm instructions to proceed with the disbursement of the deposit accordingly.

If I do not hear from you within **five working days** of this letter, the disputed sum of the claim will be passed to the relevant tenancy deposit protection scheme for adjudication and final settlement.

I look forward to your further correspondence in this matter.

Yours sincerely

Landlord: *A. Landlord*

7.6 CHASING TENANT FOR ACCEPTANCE OF PROPOSED DEDUCTIONS

A. Landlord
76–89 Alscot Road, London SE1 2EA
020 7394 4040

A. Tenant
10 Alscot Road, London SE1 3EJ

Date: *1 March 2007*

Dear *A. Tenant*

Re: *10 Alscot Road, London SE1 3EJ*

Further to my recent letter regarding the check-out that was carried out at the above-named property and my intended claim against your deposit, I am writing to advise you that I have not received a response.

I appreciate that there are circumstances where post may go missing or not be received and I therefore enclose a copy of the letter and ask that you reply accordingly.

If I do not hear from you within **five working days** of this letter, I will assume that you are happy with the claim and the deposit will be administered accordingly.

I look forward to your further correspondence in this matter.

Yours sincerely

Landlord: *A. Landlord*

7.7 DISPUTE OF CLAIM RECEIVED – DISAGREEMENT AND NOTIFICATION OF ASSIGNMENT TO TDP

A. Landlord
76–89 Alscot Road, London SE1 2EA
020 7394 4040

A. Tenant
10 Alscot Road, London SE1 3EJ

Date: *1 March 2007*

Dear *A. Tenant*

Re: *10 Alscot Road, London SE1 3EJ*

Further to my recent letter regarding the check-out that was carried out at the above-named property and my proposed deductions to be made against your deposit, I have received your correspondence in dispute of this matter.

I have considered your comments and disagree entirely with your dispute for the following reasons:

As per your signed inventory at the commencement of the tenancy, the property was not in a bad state of repair before you moved into the property. Both the armchair and the carpets were in good condition and undamaged.

I have therefore passed this matter to the tenancy deposit protection service that safeguards your deposit and requested adjudication and final settlement.

Please find enclosed a cheque for the sum of £500, being the return of the undisputed element of your deposit.

Yours sincerely

Landlord: *A. Landlord*

7.8 DISPUTE OF CLAIM RECEIVED – DISAGREEMENT

A. Landlord
76–89 Alscot Road, London SE1 2EA
020 7394 4040

A. Tenant
10 Alscot Road, London SE1 3EJ

Date: *1 March 2007*

Dear *A. Tenant*

Re: *10 Alscot Road, London SE1 3EJ*

Further to my recent letter regarding the check-out that was carried out at the above-named property and my intended deductions to be made against your deposit, I have received your correspondence in dispute of this matter.

I have considered your comments and I disagree entirely with your dispute for the following reasons:

As per your signed inventory at the commencement of the tenancy, the property was not in a bad state of repair before you moved into the property. Both the armchair and the carpets were in good condition and undamaged.

Please therefore find enclosed a cheque for the sum of £500, being the return of your deposit in respect of the above-named property minus the following deductions:

- *£100.00 – Cleaning*
- *£180.00 – Replace armchair*
- *£20.00 – Burn on carpet*

I trust that this is satisfactory and I take this opportunity to wish you all the best for your future.

Yours sincerely

Landlord: *A. Landlord*

7.9 DISPUTE OF CLAIM RECEIVED – PARTIAL AGREEMENT

A. Landlord
76–89 Alscot Road, London SE1 2EA
020 7394 4040

A. Tenant
10 Alscot Road, London SE1 3EJ

Date: *1 March 2007*

Dear *A. Tenant*

Re: *10 Alscot Road, London SE1 3EJ*

Further to my recent letter regarding the check-out that was carried out at the above-named property and my intended claim against your deposit, I have received your correspondence in dispute of the claim.

I have considered your comments and I agree in part with your reasons for disputing my claim. I am therefore happy to amend the claim as follows:

Description	Total Cost in £	Amount Claimed in £
Cleaning	100.00	100.00
Replace armchair	300.00	180.00 (3/5)
Burn on carpet	n/a	20.00 (compensation)
TOTAL	400.00	300.00

I kindly request that you confirm if you are happy for me to proceed on this basis within **five working days** of this letter.

I look forward to receiving your further correspondence in this matter.

Yours sincerely

Landlord: *A. Landlord*

7.10 DEPOSIT RETURN MINUS DEDUCTIONS

A. Landlord
76–89 Alscot Road, London SE1 2EA
020 7394 4040

A. Tenant
10 Alscot Road, London SE1 3EJ

Date: *1 March 2007*

Dear *A. Tenant*

Re: *10 Alscot Road, London SE1 3EJ*

Please find enclosed a cheque for the sum of £500, being the return of your deposit in respect of the above-named property minus the following deductions:

- *£100 – cleaning the property*
- *£150 – half towards the cost of replacing the armchair*

I trust that this is satisfactory and take this opportunity to wish you all the best for your future.

Yours sincerely

Landlord: *A. Landlord*

7.11 DEPOSIT RETURN MINUS DEDUCTIONS – AUTHORISATION SENT TO TDP

A. Landlord
76–89 Alscot Road, London SE1 2EA
020 7394 4040

A. Tenant
10 Alscot Road, London SE1 3EJ

Date: *1 March 2007*

Dear *A. Tenant*

Re: *10 Alscot Road, London SE1 3EJ*

Further to our recent communication regarding the return of your deposit in respect of the above-named property, I am writing to advise you that I have passed your authorisation to the administrator of the tenancy deposit scheme that safeguards your deposit and have requested that the following deductions be made:

- *£100 – cleaning the property*
- *£150 – half towards the cost of replacing the armchair*

I understand that a cheque will be forwarded to you within approximately ten days of receipt of the information.

I trust that this is satisfactory and I take this opportunity to wish you all the best for your future.

Yours sincerely

Landlord: *A. Landlord*

CHAPTER 8

Utility letters

At the beginning and end of each tenancy you should take meter readings at the property and inform the relevant suppliers. You should also inform the local council of the change in occupancy.

It's important to carry out this process as quickly and thoroughly as possible because failure to do so can result in demands for late payment being sent incorrectly, estimated bills which are not representative of the actual usage and lots and lots of telephone calls where you are likely to find yourself in holding queues waiting to speak to a utility supplier!

Electricity and gas

The two most common methods of measuring and calculating usage of electricity and gas are:

- a meter where you are billed on a monthly or quarterly basis; or

- a card, or key, meter which is effectively a 'pay as you go' option allowing the user to charge the card with money that can be translated into units of supply.

If your property is metered, you will need to take the readings and send them to the relevant suppliers along with the following information:

- The details of the previous person liable for the account

- Who the new account should be in the name of
- When the changeovers occurred

Your electricity meter reading may contain two numbers: one for the normal reading and another for the low reading. Do include both of these numbers when writing to the electricity supplier.

 ELECTRICITY (8.1)

The gas meter is only likely to have one reading and this should be forwarded to the gas supplier.

 GAS (8.2)

If there are card meters at the property, you should still send the above letters, but make a note on the correspondence to say that this is how the supply is provided. It's important to do this because if your tenant has a debt with a utility company, he will put the debt onto the card meter so that a little bit of money is taken each time the card is charged and put into the slot. If you fail to tell the relevant companies, you, or your new tenant, could be paying for someone else's bad credit.

> **Note**
>
> It's your tenant's right to shop around for a better deal on his electric and gas supply and you cannot prevent your tenant from changing electric or gas supplier if he wants to. It's important that you know who are the suppliers to the property and you should make sure that your tenant informs you if he does switch so that you know who to contact at the end of the tenancy.

Council Tax

There are no meter readings involved when informing the local taxation office of a change of occupancy. However, the information required by the Council Tax office is a little more detailed. In addition to the names and addresses of those no longer living at the property and the dates and details of any changes of tenancy, you will also be required to provide the following information:

- If the property is furnished or unfurnished
- If the property was or is now vacant

Properties that are vacant may be entitled to a discount, as might a property with only one occupant, so it's important to make sure that the local Council Tax office has the correct details on file.

Monthly Council Tax bills can be expensive and the local authorities are very quick these days to impose additional court charges on people who don't pay in good time. By sending correspondence quickly you can have peace of mind that you, or the previous tenant, are not being billed incorrectly.

 COUNCIL TAX (8.3)

Water and sewerage

Historically, water and sewerage supplies were operated by the same company, but this is less frequently the case today. If the companies are separate, you should ensure that both are notified of the change of occupants at the property.

Newer properties are more likely to have water meters installed which are easy to get to and if your property is equipped with one of these, you should note the reading and inform the relevant supplier accordingly.

Alternatively, if your property doesn't have a meter or you are unable to get to the meter because of its location, it's acceptable to send correspondence to the supplier that informs them of the standard changes in occupants along with the corresponding dates.

 WATER (8.4)

SEWERAGE (8.5)

8.1 ELECTRICITY

A. Landlord
76–89 Alscot Road, London SE1 2EA
020 7394 4040

A. Electricity Co.
24 Lightning Way, London W19 7UP

Date: *1 September 2007*

Dear *A. Electricity*

Re: *10 Alscot Road, London SE1 3EJ*

I am writing to advise you, as owners of the above-named property, that a change of occupiers has taken place as follows:

Date of Change of Occupancy: *1 August 2007*

Meter Reading: _____ (low) _____ (normal)

Name and Forwarding Address for Previous Account: *A. Tenant, 92 High Street, London SW17 2AV*

New Account Name: *A. Tenant 2*

Please can you amend your records accordingly.

Yours sincerely

Landlord: *A. Landlord*

8.2 GAS

A. Landlord
76–89 Alscot Road, London SE1 2EA
020 7394 4040

A. Gas Co.
52 Meter Way, London E19 4RA

Date: *1 September 2007*

Dear *A. Gas*

Re: *10 Alscot Road, London SE1 3EJ*

I am writing to advise you, as owners of the above-named property, that a change of occupiers has taken place as follows:

Date of Change of Occupancy: *1 August 2007*

Meter Reading: _____

Name and Forwarding Address for Previous Account: *A. Tenant, 92 High Street, London SW17 2AV*

New Account Name: *A. Tenant 2*

Please can you amend your records accordingly.

Yours sincerely

Landlord: *A. Landlord*

8.3 COUNCIL TAX

A. Landlord
76–89 Alscot Road, London SE1 2EA
020 7394 4040

A. London Council
71 Government Road, London NW9 7AP

Date: *1 September 2007*

Dear *A. Council*

Re: *10 Alscot Road, London SE1 3EJ*

I am writing to advise you, as owners of the above-named property, that a change of occupiers has taken place as follows:

Date of Change of Occupancy: *1 August 2007*

Name and Forwarding Address for Previous Account: *A. Tenant, 92 High Street, London SW17 2AV*

New Account Name: *A. Tenant 2*

The Property is: *Unfurnished*

The Property is Currently: *Occupied*

Please can you amend your records accordingly.

Yours sincerely

Landlord: *A. Landlord*

8.4 WATER

A. Landlord
76–89 Alscot Road, London SE1 2EA
020 7394 4040

A. Water Co.
21 River Road, London E2 9AP

Date: *1 September 2007*

Dear *A. Water*

Re: *10 Alscot Road, London SE1 3EJ*

I am writing to advise you, as owners of the above-named property, that a change of occupiers has taken place as follows:

Date of Change of Occupancy: *1 August 2007*

Meter Reading: _____ (if applicable)

Name and Forwarding Address for Previous Account: *A. Tenant, 92 High Street, London SW17 2AV*

New Account Name: *A. Tenant 2*

Please can you amend your records accordingly.

Yours sincerely

Landlord: *A. Landlord*

8.5 SEWERAGE

A. Landlord
76–89 Alscot Road, London SE1 2EA
020 7394 4040

A. Sewerage Co.
54 Stream Lane, London SW2 9RN

Date: *1 September 2007*

Dear *A. Sewerage*

Re: *10 Alscot Road, London SE1 3EJ*

I am writing to advise you, as owners of the above-named property, that a change of occupiers has taken place as follows:

Date of Change of Occupancy: *1 August 2007*

Name and Forwarding Address for Previous Account: *A. Tenant, 92 High Street, London SW17 2AV*

New Account Name: *A. Tenant 2*

Please can you amend your records accordingly.

Yours sincerely

Landlord: *A. Landlord*

CHAPTER 9

Directory

Advice

Citizens Advice

Myddelton House
115–123 Pentonville Road
London N1 9LZ

Tel: 020 7833 2181 (*admin only*)
Website: www.adviceguide.org.uk

Arbitration

Chartered Institute of Arbitrators

International Arbitration and
Mediation Centre
12 Bloomsbury Square
London WC1A 2LP

Tel: 020 7421 7444
Email: info@arbitrators.org
Website: www.arbitrators.org

Building

Federation of Master Builders

Gordon Fisher House
14–15 Great James Street
London WC1N 3DP

Tel: 020 7242 7583
Website: www.fmb.org.uk

Court Service

Her Majesty's Court Service

Customer Service Unit
5th Floor
Clive House
Petty France
London SW1H 9HD

Tel: 020 7189 2000/0845 456 8770
Email: customerservicecshq@
hmcourts-service.gsi.gov.uk
Website: www.hmcourts-service.
gov.uk

Craftsmen

Guild of Master Craftsmen

166 High Street
Lewes BN7 1XU

Tel: 01273 478 449
Email: theguild@thegmcgroup.com
Website: www.thegmcgroup.com/
theguild

Credit reporting

Equifax

Capital House
25 Chapel Street
London NW1 5DS

Website: www.equifax.co.uk

Experian

Talbot House
Talbot Street
Nottingham NG80 1TH

Website: www.experian.co.uk

Decorating

Painting and Decorating Association

32 Coton Road

Tel: 024 7635 3776

Nuneaton
Warwickshire CV11 5TW

Email: info@painting
decoratingassociation.co.uk
Website: www.painting
decoratingassociation.co.uk

Electrical (and safety)

National Inspection Council for Electrical Installation Contracting
(NICEIC)

Warwick House
Houghton Hall Park
Houghton Regis, Dunstable
Bedfordshire LU5 5ZX

Tel: 01582 531 000
Email: enquiries@niceic.com
Website: www.niceic.org.uk

Environmental protection

National Society for Clean Air (& Environmental Protection)

44 Grand Parade
Brighton
East Sussex BN2 9QA

Tel: 01273 878 770
Website: www.nsca.org.uk

Estate agents

National Association of Estate Agents

Arbon House
21 Jury Street
Warwick CV34 4EH

Tel: 01926 496 800
Email: info@naea.co.uk
Website: www.naea.co.uk

Fire safety

Fire Kills, Government Advice Website

Fire Kills

Website: www.firekills.gov.uk

Gardening

Aboricultural Association

Ampfield House	Tel: 0179 436 8717
Romsey	Email: admin@trees.org.uk
Hampshire SO51 9PA	Website: www.trees.org.uk

Gas (and safety)

CORGI (Council for Registered Gas Installers)

1 Elmwood	Tel: 0870 401 2200
Chineham Park	Email: enquiries@trustcorgi.com
Crockford Lane	Website: www.trustcorgi.com/
Basingstoke	consumers.htmx
Hampshire RG24 8WG	

Health and Safety Executive's Office

Tel: 0845 345 0055	Website: www.hse.gov.uk/gas

Transco/The National Grid

National Grid House	Tel: 0845 605 6677 (*enquiries*)
Warwick Technology Park	Tel: 0800 111 999 (*24-hour gas*
Gallows Hill	*leak reporting*)
Warwick CV34 6DA	Website: www.nationalgrid.com

Hazardous materials

Asbestos

Health and Safety Executive's Office

Tel: 0845 345 0055	Website: www.hse.gov.uk/
	asbestos

Radon

Health Protection Agency

Centre for Radiation, Chemical and Environmental Hazards Chilton Didcot Oxon OX11 0RQ	Tel: 01235 831 600 Email: rpd@hpa-rp.org.uk Website: www.hpa.org.uk/ radiation

Insurance

HomeLet

HomeLet Becor House Green Lane Lincoln LN6 7DL	Tel: 0844 561 0660 Email: enquiry@homelet.co.uk Website: www.homelet.co.uk

Letsure

Lumley Letsure Ltd Hargrave House Belmont Road Maidenhead Berkshire SL6 6TB	Tel: 0870 077 0660 Email: info@letsure.co.uk Website: www.letsure.co.uk

Landlord organisations

National Landlords Association

22–26 Albert Embankment London SE1 7TJ	Tel: 020 7840 8900 Email: info@landlords.org.uk Website: www.landlords.org.uk

Locksmiths

Master Locksmiths Association

5D Great Central Way Woodford Halse Daventry NN11 3PZ	Tel: 0800 783 1498 Email: enquiries@locksmiths. co.uk Website: www.locksmiths.co.uk

Neighbourhood watch

Neighbourhood Watch

Home Office Direct Communications Unit 2 Marsham Street London SW1P 4DF	Tel: 020 7035 4848 Email: public.enquiries@home office.gsi.gov.uk Website: www.neighbourhood watch.uk.com

Noise pollution

National Society for Clean Air (& Environmental Protection)

44 Grand Parade Brighton East Sussex BN2 9QA	Tel: 01273 878 770 Website: www.nsca.org.uk

Noise Abatement Society

Flat 2 26 Brunswick Terrace Hove East Sussex BN3 1HJ	Tel: 01273 823 851 Email: nas@noiseabatement society.fsnet.co.uk Website: www.noiseabatement society.com

Plumbing and central heating

Association of Plumbing and Heating Contractors

14 Ensign House	Tel: 024 7647 0626
Ensign Business Centre	Fax: 024 7647 0942
Westwood Way	Website: www.aphc.co.uk
Coventry CV4 8JA	

Institute of Plumbing and Heating Engineering

64 Station Lane	Tel: 01708 472 791
Hornchurch	Email: info@iphe.org.uk
Essex RM12 6NB	Website: www.iphe.org.uk

Roofing

National Federation of Roofing Contractors

24 Weymouth Street	Tel: 020 7436 0387
London W1G 7LX	Website: www.nfrc.co.uk

Index